LOUISIANA CRAWFISH

LOUISIANA CRAWFISH

A SUCCULENT HISTORY OF THE CAJUN CRUSTACEAN

SAM IRWIN

Foreword by MARCELLE BIENVENU

AMERICAN PALATE

Published by American Palate
A Division of The History Press
Charleston, SC 29403
www.historypress.net

Copyright © 2014 by Sam Irwin
All rights reserved

First published 2014

Manufactured in the United States

ISBN 978.1.62619.236.2

Library of Congress CIP data applied for.

For Joe and Mathilde Amy and Robert K. Irwin

CONTENTS

A CRAWFISH TALE

I remember (I really do) the first time I laid eyes on a live crawfish. I was riding shotgun in Papa's Chevy pickup truck heading to Catahoula, a fishing community in St. Martin Parish located just outside the levee system that contains the Atchafalaya Basin (also known as the Atchafalaya Swamp).

Papa and I often stole away in the pickup to go on great adventures around the parish. You see, Papa was the publisher/editor of our local weekly newspaper, the *Teche News*, and he took me with him on "his route" to collect the coins in the many newspaper stands that were located outside of just about every grocery store, bait shop and café in St. Martin Parish.

That particular day, our first stop was at Mr. Laviolette's. This was a place I had never been before. A putt-putt boat, called *le bateau* by the locals, was pulled onto the banks of Catahoula Lake, where two boys about my age were hosing down the cypress watercraft. Cypress was the wood of choice for basin fishermen's boats.

"*Comment ça va?*" Mr. Laviolette greeted us.

"*Ça va,*" Papa responded.

They continued their chat while I walked gingerly down the oyster-shell driveway to see what the boys were up to. As I approached, one of them reached into a bucket and pulled out a small, squiggling... something. It wasn't a crab, nor was it any kind of fish. It kind of looked like a shrimp—but no, it had little claws. The boy shoved it right to the tip of my nose. I screeched! The boys howled with laughter.

Papa and Mr. Laviolette looked over to see what was causing such a commotion.

Papa gathered me up by one hairy arm—the other held an ice-cold beer—and shushed me.

"T-Black." (My father's name is Marcel, and I was named after him. His nickname was Blackie, so I became T-Black.) "It's only an *écrevisse*, a crawfish. Mr. Laviolette is giving us a sack of them to take home for a crawfish boil."

Our bounty was chucked into the back of the pickup, and we headed home.

In our big backyard, shaded with ancient live oaks, the crawfish were dumped into a large metal tub to be cleaned and purged. After Papa dug into his ever-present ice chest for a cold beer, he showed me how to hold a crawfish so its claws couldn't pinch me. While we set about our task readying the little crustaceans for our boil, Papa told me this story:

> *A very, very long time ago, the lobster and the Acadians resided happily together in what is now Nova Scotia in Canada. Then the Acadians were cruelly expelled from their beloved land and wandered for years searching for a home, some finally settling in the bayous of southern Louisiana. The lobsters yearned for their French friends and set out off across the country to find them. The journey south was so long and arduous that they began to shrink in size. And now we have these,* chère, *an almost perfect miniature of a lobster, and they are called crawfish.*

Ever since that day, *Monsieur Écrevisse* and I have been very good friends.

Who would have known that these small freshwater crustaceans would become a multimillion-dollar industry?

In the 1950s, most of the crawfish came from the Atchafalaya Basin. Fishermen would bring in their catch, keep what they needed to feed their families and then peddle the rest to their friends and neighbors for pennies a pound. They were considered a "poor man's food," and boy, was I happy we were "poor." Just about every Friday of my childhood, when we had to abstain from eating meat in our Catholic community, Papa had big pots of crawfish (and sometimes shrimp or crabs) boiling in the backyard. The boiling water was seasoned with a copious amount of salt and cayenne pepper, and potatoes, onions and corn on the cob were added to the pot to "stretch" the meal. Oh my, those were some of the best times.

Everyone would stand elbow to elbow around the big picnic table that had been "dressed" with layers of old newspapers and pinch, peel and suck mountains of crawfish, munch on the perfectly seasoned vegetables and wash it all down with cold beer (root beers for the youngsters). (I remember my mother warning me not to eat boiled crawfish in front of people we didn't know else they would think we were barbarians—all that pinching, peeling and sucking going on.)

But in 1959, our world of crawfish consuming was about to change big time. The town of Breaux Bridge decided to celebrate its centennial by having a crawfish festival of all things. People were eating boiled crawfish out of paper bags—on the street for goodness sake. There was even a crawfish queen! (I would have joined the competition, but only girls from Breaux Bridge could participate.)

All of a sudden, crawfish were cool! People were coming from "away" to eat crawfish. Crawfishermen were on a roll. Sacks of crawfish (about forty pounds) went for about twenty-five dollars. By the 1960s, peeling plants sprung up in the communities along the Atchafalaya levee system to supply peeled tails with which to make étouffée, bisque, pies, boulettes and anything else conjured up by the resourceful Cajuns. During the crawfish season, which back then ran from January to June, sacks of live crawfish and bags of peeled tails were exported to markets in Houston and New Orleans.

Where were all these crawfish coming from? According to the LSU AgCenter,

> up until that time, most of the crawfish available for people to consume had come from wild harvests in natural habitats. Although crawfish were very abundant some years due to high water levels in the Atchafalaya Basin and other natural wetland areas, in other years crawfish were scarce and difficult to come by. This variation in supply made it difficult for markets to grow. Once crawfish farming began, it allowed for more consistent supplies from year to year. By the mid-1960s, the amount of land devoted to crawfish farming had increased to approximately 7,000 acres of managed ponds. At this point, an industry based on peeling crawfish became established, and the new markets for crawfish meat allowed both crawfish farming and wild harvests to increase even more. Acreage continued to increase in Louisiana, from approximately 44,000 acres in the mid-1970s to current levels of roughly 185,000 acres.

After the harvesting of the pond crawfish (roughly from December to April), the ponds can then be used for rice farming, thus providing farmers with a yearlong income. (Hey, I told you Cajuns are innovative.)

But as usual, there is a trade-off. The popularity of crawfish and the increased cost of operating crawfish/rice ponds have caused an inflation of the price of both live crawfish and peeled tails. But that hasn't deterred the growth of the industry. After all, life in south Louisiana just wouldn't be worth living without a weekly crawfish boil during crawfish season. Heck, on Good Friday, one would be hard-pressed to find someone *not* enjoying mounds of crawfish—pinching, peeling and sucking!

There are so many stories and tales to tell about the evolution of the mighty crawfish, and who better to enlighten the reader of the history and the many nuances of that small crustacean than Sam Irwin, a native of Breaux Bridge who has chronicled his experiences in this tome. Grab a beer (or whatever is your poison), sit back, make yourself comfortable and find out why crawfish has become so important to our foodways and culture in south Louisiana. I promise you a good read!

MARCELLE BIENVENU
"The Queen of Cajun Cooking"

ACKNOWLEDGEMENTS

This book was made possible with the cooperation of Betty Dupont, Simone Irwin, Grace Amy Irwin, Carl and Renella Simon, James Avault Jr., Robert Romaire, Jay Huner, Cynthia Roberthon Guidry, the Crawfish Festival Association, Harris Pellerin Jr., Pat Huval, Agnes Huval, Terry Guidry, Rocky Landry, Emily Beck Cogburn, Tom Sweat, Henri Bienvenu, Marcelle Bienvenu, Ken Grissom, Sally Angelle, the *Teche News* and the unsung heroes who scanned all of the Baton Rouge/New Orleans newspapers and put them online into digitized form. Also, Barbara Trahan Broussard, Roland Faulk, Robert Les Domingues, Jim Fowler, Roy Johnson, David Cheramie (for checking my French grammar), Bert Tietje, Ray Pellerin, Robyn Underwood, Darlene from the Sam Houston Regional Library, the Louisiana Department of Agriculture and Forestry, the LSU AgCenter Aquaculture Research Station and all who responded to my call for crawfish stories and history.

Special thanks goes to photographer Ron J. Berard, who provided endless technical assistance and some outstanding photos.

CHAPTER 1

THE CAJUN CRUSTACEAN

My grandfather Joe Amy (pronounced *Ah-me*) of Henderson was a pioneer in the crawfish business. His boat navigated the Atchafalaya River in the 1920s and bought fish directly from fishermen who lived in Butte la Rose, Atchafalaya Station, Pelba and other river communities. Catfish, buffalo carp and *casse burgot* (gaspergou) were shipped via the Southern Pacific Rail Line that crossed the Atchafalaya Swamp to the urban centers east and west of the Mississippi River. Because of refrigeration storage issues, crawfish as a commercial product was an afterthought in the first half of the twentieth century.[1]

But that doesn't mean crawfish weren't available. Crawfish were plentiful (and just as delicious) in the 1920s as they are today, but the markets were supplied locally.

"Crawfish are to be had at any [New Orleans] restaurant in town, prepared in a variety of ways. Half of the crawfish eaten in New Orleans, however, are not bought but caught by the children of a family for amusement, if living in a crawfish section," wrote Carleton Pool of the Louisiana Department of Conservation in a 1923 *Times-Picayune* article.[2]

To the delight of residents who live on Hagen Avenue, a block off western Orleans Avenue, the street was a crawfish section, and crawfish could be caught in backyard wetlands. Families often went on crawfish picnics or bought boiled crawfish on the street. A wet New Orleans was a crawfish paradise. An anonymous Works Progress Administration writer described the crawfish habits of the Crescent City in the *Brief History of Creole Cooking in New Orleans*:

Joe and Mathilde Amy sit on the porch of their store in Henderson. Amy's Fisheries received a permit to peel crawfish for retail and restaurant use in 1954. *Grace Amy Irwin.*

Native Orleanians are naturally very fond of seafood, and they will drive miles to partake of any well-seasoned dish of this delicacy. At West End, a park situated on Lake Pontchartrain, there are numerous stands which specialize in the serving of boiled crabs and shrimp. In the warm weather, tables are placed along the seawall, and nothing is more enjoyable on a warm night or after a swim in the lake than to ride to one of these places and feast on this specialty. On certain nights, (usually Thursday, Friday and Saturday) many bars serve free crabs, shrimp and crayfish with the purchase of a glass of beer or any other drink.[3]

Consumers became alarmed as New Orleans's wetlands were drained to create more neighborhoods and the picnickers aghast at having to travel by car to far-off Crescent City lands like Shrewsbury, Gentilly, St. Bernard or Kenner for their crawfish fix.[4]

Even though Pool reported that "many old residents declare[d] that crawfish lose much of their flavor unless accompanied by a bottle of *vin rouge*" and that Prohibition "destroyed much of the attractiveness and delight of timbale of crawfish,"[5] crawfish were "always a big deal in the New Orleans area"[6] and had the power to bring big-city sportswriters like William McG. Keefe to tears.

Keefe confessed that he existed "all year to live during the crawfish season," and a prediction of a light crawfish year for 1931 was "sufficient cause for deep, sincere grief…to think there'll be a shortsy on them this season! Weeps, weeps, weeps!"[7]

Crawfish was also a big deal in the Assumption Parish community of Pierre Part. "During the summer there is an abundance of crabs, and in the spring, of crawfish. For the families, this is just another variety of fish," wrote Father Herman J. Jacobi in his study of the Louisiana Catholic family.[8]

Without mentioning the merchant's name, Jacobi made note of a seafood canning plant at Pierre Part, begun in 1932 "as an experiment in supplying local and distant markets with canned turtle-soup, crawfish bisque and refrigerated crab meat. In 1936 he packed over 1,000 cases of his products, 24 cans to the case, and shipped over 5,000 pounds of crab meat. He barely made expenses for three years and then realized some profit by 1936."[9]

In 1922, the year before Pool penned "Vast Commercial Possibilities of the Humble Louisiana Crawfish" for the *Times-Picayune*, Louisiana's crawfish catch was 7,265 pounds.[10] The industry had nowhere to go but up as the state's transportation grid improved. Ironically, the construction of Airline Highway from Baton Rouge to New Orleans ruined the fisheries west of New Orleans and opened up the Atchafalaya Basin crawfish to the largest metropolitan area in the state.[11]

But crawfish had the biggest impact on St. Martin Parish. The real thrust of the modern crawfish industry—that is, the business that provided fresh, peeled crawfish tail meat to restaurants—grew from the western side of the Atchafalaya Basin because a man named Henry Guidry used

Guidry's Place endured flooding, but Henderson became a center of Cajun crawfish cuisine when Pat Huval sold the old dancehall and built Pat's Waterfront Restaurant on Bayou Amy. *Pat Huval.*

a team of mules to move his seafood restaurant away from the farming community of Lenora, six miles east of Breaux Bridge, to the foot of the West Atchafalaya River Protection Levee, thus founding the town of Henderson in 1934.

Pat Huval, the famous brash-talking restaurateur of Pat's Fisherman's Wharf in Henderson, makes no bones about it. Every menu he has ever printed proudly proclaims Henderson (and by extension, Guidry's Place and Huval's restaurants) as the place "where it all began." A compelling case can be made to support Huval's bold statement.

Henderson's claim can be traced to an improbable chain of events dating back to the 1755 expulsion of the Acadians from Canada's Maritime Provinces by the English. The deportation was a consequence of the French and Indian War, also known as the Seven Years' War. The exile, termed *Le Grand Dérangement*, created a "collective historical ordeal which served to bind the people [Cajuns] together years, centuries even, after the event was concluded."[12]

The expelled Acadians who settled in Louisiana came to be known as Cajuns. Many Cajuns, insulated by choice with their Catholic religion and French language, tended to disassociate from Louisiana-born French Creoles and the Protestant Americans who poured into Louisiana after the colony became a state in 1812. The Cajuns who lived along Bayou Teche and Bayou Lafourche disliked going into debt and readily sold their land to well-financed sugarcane planters to avoid paying taxes and levee-building fees. Many moved into the smaller bayou valleys that drained the Atchafalaya River and began farming.[13]

They would have continued to farm, but Captain Henry Shreve cleared a large, impenetrable raft of driftwood at the upper end of the Atchafalaya near present-day Simmesport in 1831 and changed the Atchafalaya River hydrology.[14] Cajun farmland now became Cajun swamp as the river's annual spring rise became more severe and flooded agricultural land. The farmers adapted by becoming fishermen.[15] But their waterfront lifestyle based on timber, alligator, fish, turtle, fur and crawfish extraction was altered again in 1928 when Congress passed the Flood Control Act and the U.S. Army Corps of Engineers created the Atchafalaya Spillway.[16] The spillway, also called the Atchafalaya Basin or Atchafalaya Floodway, was designed to divert overflow water from the Mississippi and Red Rivers down the Atchafalaya River into a holding channel twenty miles wide to protect the lower Mississippi River Valley from a devastating flood like the one that occurred in 1927.[17]

After the spillway was created, annual flood levels along the Atchafalaya River and its distributaries were more severe. The already demanding swamp life, as noble as it sounds, was without electricity, a good supply of clean drinking water and basic medical services. Now flooding was more frequent and severe. Life in Butte la Rose, Bayou Chene, Pelba, Atchafalaya Station, Happy Town, Graine a Volee Cove, Bayou Crook Creek, Starvation Town and Big Pass was even harder.[18]

As a child, Sosthene Amy, a current resident of Henderson, attended the school at Butte la Rose, to which river children were bussed by boat. Amy said the doors to the schoolhouse were left open every spring to let rising floodwaters flow through the school. "The boys had to shovel out the sand after the water went down," Amy said.

Shoveling silt and removing hissing serpents, reptiles, amphibians and wildlife from one's river home on an annual basis was a prospect few wanted to continually endure. The Cajun swamp dwellers and other smaller ethnic groups who had lived on the river highways for a century moved to towns outside the spillway levees for washing machines, refrigerators, schools and doctors.[19] They moved alongside Henry Guidry in Henderson and to communities like Catahoula and Coteau Homes on the basin's western edge. Others settled in Pierre Part, Belle River and

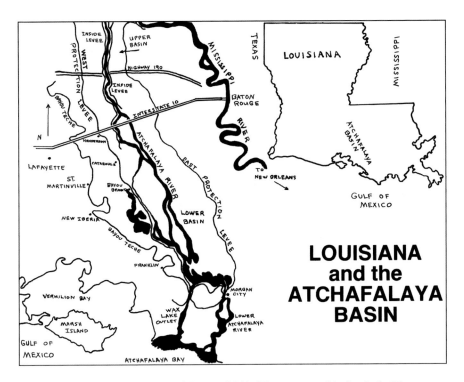

Most of the early commercial crawfish crop (1940–80) was trapped in the Atchafalaya Basin, but farm-raised crawfish is the major source for crawfish today. *Greg Guirard.*

Bayou Pigeon on the eastern side. English speakers relocated to Bayou Sorrel, also on the eastern side. Butte la Rose is the only town that exists inside the Atchafalaya Basin today.[20]

The new Henderson Landing community was composed mostly of commercial fishermen and fish buyers who could readily supply crawfish to the growing market. A new road, present-day Louisiana Highway 352, was built by the U.S. Army Corps of Engineers and created easy access to the "gateway to the Atchafalaya."[21] The advent of the outboard boat motor popularized sport fishing, and Henderson Lake, seventeen miles from Lafayette, became an important recreational fishing location.[22] Commercial boat landings were established on the lakeside of the spillway levee, and numerous "camps" and houseboats became homes away from home for many sportsmen. A sizable weekend crowd partied at Guidry's Place and other dancehall/restaurants that sprung up in the new community. Interestingly enough, Guidry's Place and the competing Talley's Place, which remained in Lenora, did not openly offer crawfish on their menus.[23]

Crawfish was easily obtained in the area by anyone willing to wade through the water with a seine net or a *carrelet* (a net attached to the end of a pole). The Hebert Hotel in Breaux Bridge and Guidroz's (also written as Guittreaux's) were well-known establishments that served crawfish as early as the 1920s. But crawfish dishes involved quite a bit of preparation (one had to peel about one hundred pounds of crawfish to obtain fifteen pounds of meat), and disposal of the waste was another obstacle to overcome. That may be the reason the crawfish-peeling industry was slow to take off, but the people who caught them knew how to cook them, and word of good food travels well by word of mouth. In any event, crawfish dishes already popular in Cajun homes became extremely popular in the Henderson and Breaux Bridge restaurants after World War II.[24]

Pat and Agnes Huval bought Guidry's Place in 1954 but quickly sold it to Harris LeBlanc to build a restaurant—no dancehall necessary to attract customers.[25] "More and more they were coming to eat," Huval said. "The people really liked my food."[26] Robin's Dancehall also began to serve crawfish.

Mary White, a waitress at Robin's, taught many a Lafayette visitor how to enjoy crawfish. "I worked as a waitress at Robin's Seafood in Henderson during the early 1950s," White said. "I witnessed the uncertainty customers had about eating these little bugs. I helped many folks peel crawfish and then convinced them how nutritious the other crawfish dishes were."[27]

Another important factor in why the tiny community of Henderson became the first major player in the crawfish industry was labor. The migration from the interior of the Atchafalaya River swamp created the labor force necessary for the tedious job of crawfish peeling. The wives and children of the commercial fishermen peeled crawfish by the pound and earned cash money.

But crawfish also created a labor market, and employable women from the nearby rural communities of Nina, Grand Anse, Cecilia, Arnaudville and Breaux Bridge could earn cash money. African American women also peeled crawfish alongside their white counterparts and contributed to the crawfish economy.[28]

In 1973, Interstate 10's 18.2-mile Atchafalaya Basin Bridge connecting Lafayette to Baton Rouge opened, and the daily traffic count that passed by the fishing village went from 0 to 7,390 overnight. Ten years later, the traffic count was 26,472, and Henderson boasted not one but four to five restaurants that specialized in crawfish cuisine.[29] "When they opened up

Interstate 10, it was like God came down from heaven," said Agnes Huval, Pat Huval's former wife.[30]

Baton Rouge was only forty minutes from the freshest crawfish—Lafayette's oilmen and their hefty expense accounts were only twenty minutes away. Horsemen, flush with cash from their winnings at Evangeline Downs, could share their good luck with trainers, jockeys, girlfriends and high rollers at Henderson's famous crawfish inns. Water plane pilots even landed their aircraft in Bayou Amy to entertain their clients at Pat's. The tiny town of Henderson, incorporated in 1971, was truly the "town that crawfish built."[31] The four restaurants could seat more than three thousand epicureans at any given time.[32]

The first permit to peel crawfish and sell the meat was not issued to a Henderson merchant but to Abby Latiolais of Catahoula in 1949. Within a few months, Berthemost Montet of Henderson had started peeling crawfish and was followed by Joe Amy, Aristile Robin and Freddie Zerangue, also of Henderson. Their customers were the growing number of restaurants that featured crawfish in season.[33] Lafayette restaurants like Don's Seafood

Mim Blanchard of Mim's Café in Breaux Bridge cooks crawfish in 1959. Mim's was a popular meeting place for the early Crawfish Festival planners. *Ashton Roberthon family.*

and Steakhouse, Vermilion Inn, Poor Boy's Riverside Inn and the Half-Shell needed fresh crawfish meat.[34] Don's quickly expanded to Baton Rouge, New Orleans, Morgan City and Beaumont (Texas) and brought fresh-peeled crawfish meat, the basis for Cajun haute cuisine, to the oilfield, legislators in Baton Rouge and old Creoles in New Orleans. Piccadilly Cafeteria in Baton Rouge wanted crawfish for its serving line by the mid-1950s, and its crawfish étouffée recipe became "the most successful recipe we ever had."[35]

Other restaurants like Mim's Café, the Rendezvous Club, Mulate's, Theresa's and Thelma's in Breaux Bridge featured crawfish. By the mid-1960s, the increasingly celebrated crawfish replaced the Basin's fish economy. By 1989, probably the height of the crawfish-peeling industry, twenty crawfish-peeling plants within a two-mile radius of Amy's Fisheries were in business, including Amy's Fisheries, Atchafalaya Crawfish Processors, Basin Crawfish Processors, Bayou Land Seafood, Bonanza Crawfish, Fisherman's Pier Seafood, Hayes Fisheries, Huval's Seafood, La Louisiane Seafood, Las's Crawfish Plant, Seafood Inc., Cajun Country Crawfish, Cajun Seafood Distributors, Henderson Fisheries, Pat's Waterfront Seafood Packing Plant and Schexnider Crawfish.[36] Catahoula, six miles away, had nine processors,

Early crawfish processors used whatever equipment they had at their disposal before investing too heavily in the fledgling crawfish industry. This boiling room was part of Chez Sidney's Catahoula operation. *Courtesy* Teche News.

including Pete Guidry, Chez Sidney and Clearwater Crawfish, while Coteau Holmes had three, including the Dalton and Allen Dugas plants.[37]

I witnessed this crawfish paradigm shift through my adolescence. Later, as a college student and after, I worked at Amy's Fisheries from 1972 to 1984, first as a laborer and deliveryman and then as a crawfish buyer and manager. My parents, Bob and Grace Irwin of Breaux Bridge, worked in the crawfish industry and were also officers of the Breaux Bridge Crawfish Festival Association, which promoted the lowly crawfish to the world with tremendous success. My sisters all promoted crawfish in their own ways. Kathy served as maid to the Crawfish Queen of 1968. Cindy was a member of the inaugural 1968 Écrevettes, an ambassadorial mid-teen dance group. Susan was both the Junior Crawfish Queen and Crawfish Queen. Carolyn and I rode on floats in the 1964 Crawfish Festival Parade, and I also marched in the parade as a member of the Breaux Bridge High School Band from 1969 to 1972. Years later, I became press secretary of the Louisiana Department of Agriculture and Forestry and served as public relations advisor to the Louisiana Crawfish Promotion and Research Board. My ties to the crawfish industry are deep, as deep as a crawfish hole.

Louisiana residents, especially those who call themselves Cajuns, are prone to "catching" a variety of ailments and/or misfortunes. Of course, anyone can catch a cold, but a Cajun can "catch a heart attack" as easily as he can "catch a flat tire." We can also catch positive things. We can "catch some good luck" or "catch an ace in a *bourrée* game."

In the springtime, Cajuns catch an *envie* (a sudden desire) for crawfish. An envie (pronounced *ahn-vee*) makes us do extraordinary things. When a resident of south Louisiana "catches an envie" for a crawfish boil, he will move heaven and earth to find a squirming sackful.

Urges to host crawfish boils are often caught on Friday evenings or Saturday afternoons, three-day weekends or Sunday family reunions. And when you telephone "momma and them" to come over for the crawfish boil, you've got to have the crawfish—big ones. Sometimes finding suitable crawfish is as easy as a trip to the grocery store. Sometimes crawfish are so plentiful that the price drops overnight. But sometimes crawfish cannot be had even for ten dollars a pound because of a cold snap, too much rain, not enough rain or the fact that *Américains* (anyone not Cajun) from Houston bought them all.

Urbanites will gather about seafood markets specializing in boiled crawfish for hours, waiting for the day's catch to come in. They'll pay top dollar for a well-seasoned three-pound serving of the tasty crustacean. Otherwise sophisticated adults will endure line cutters, heat and humidity, mosquitoes, high gas prices and everything short of murder to procure crawfish for their families' backyard boils or companies' corporate picnics.

It's "crawfish chic" to have a clandestine crawfish connection. You casually disclose that you either "know an old Cajun" or that you have a friend or a third cousin who has a direct relationship with an Atchafalaya River swamper or a crawfish farmer from Acadia Parish. Maybe it's a friend of a friend who owns a seafood market, someone who works a crawfish boiling rig in the parking lot of a Piggly Wiggly or a waiter who once took orders in a French Quarter po' boy shop.

The hunt for red crawfish is the raison d'être of Acadian spring. Phone calls will be made. Surreptitious texts will arrive on the smartphone in the wee hours. Favors will be called in. Deals will be struck, and treks to far-off crawfish ponds in rural areas will ensue. Cash money will exchange hands. No less than blood, sweat and tears will be shed in the quest for crawfish.

Rural residents, who mistakenly believe that catching crawfish is easy, scoff at their less enterprising urban cousins. They'll get the dip nets from the wash houses, steal momma's chicken livers and gizzards from the freezer for bait, rouse the kids and skip out in the early morning. A wooded and watery drainage canal must be found (not too hard in south Louisiana) to set their dip nets in. The rest of the day will be spent walking along a lonely country road to repeatedly check each net. The crawfish trapping session usually ends when a five-gallon bucket is filled or daddy gets tired of slapping at horse flies and shooing mud daubers away from the kids.

Why go through all the trouble? The answer is simple: nothing tastes as viscerally succulent as the tail meat from a big-claw crawfish. Nothing looks as beautiful as a table lined with yesterday's *Morning Advocate* piled high with bright-red boiled crawfish punctuated with onions, corn or potatoes. Crawfish satisfy almost every primal desire and cure a craving you didn't even know you had. You've had to lift and tote, wash and clean, season, boil and peel the hard shell away from every singular bit of plump umami protein. That tiny curled bit of juicy crawfish meat that you have wrested from nature and now hold in your fingers is the culmination of the expedition, the hunt and the push-and-shove sacrifice you endured to create this beautiful mess for your family and friends.

You've done it all. You've conquered nature. You stand before your peers and think, "I created this feast"—and then some yahoo says, "I think the crawfish need more salt." The crawfish boil is a south Louisiana phenomenon that now approaches the level of sacred ritual.

So who delivered crawfish to the masses? There are many contributors. Some have had their heyday, and some are yet to reach their potential. But if you like crawfish, these are the people you have to thank:

THE CAJUNS

The Cajuns as a group, especially those who lived in and along the edges of the Atchafalaya River Basin and other water bodies, retained their language, religion and culture since the first group of Acadians came to Poste des Attakapas, present-day St. Martin Parish, in 1765.[38] They also retained their foodways. Their cuisine "tends to be a richly inventive and creative one, but fundamentally it is a cuisine of a people who are reliant on themselves and the products of their own farms and rivers and surrounding forests for sustenance."[39]

THE ATCHAFALAYA RIVER

Crawfish could practically be scooped up with a *carrelet* (pole net) and were there for the taking[40] well into the 1970s. They were a cheap but readily available food source in the spring for the swamp dwellers.[41] The Atchafalaya Spillway, also called the floodway and now generally referred to as the Atchafalaya Basin, was the main source for crawfish until the 1980s.

THE BREAUX BRIDGE CRAWFISH FESTIVAL

This spring festival, which was spawned by the bayou town's 1959 centennial celebration, has been promoting the crawfish for fifty-four years. The politics of hosting a downtown festival were a spectator sport until 1993, when the city council finally banished the party to Parc Hardy.

THE RESTAURANTS

Restaurants like Pat's Waterfront, Las's, Robin's (pronounced *Roe-ban*) and Charlie's Hut in Henderson, Thelma's, Theresa's, Mim's Café, Breaux's One-Stop, the Hebert Hotel, Guittreaux's and Mulate's in Breaux Bridge, the Yellow Bowl in Jeanerette, Don's Seafood and Steakhouse, Vermilion

"Crawfish Dishes Our Specialty" was the calling card of the place settings at Mim's Café in Breaux Bridge. *Ashton Roberthon family.*

Inn and Po-Boy's Riverside Inn in Lafayette and Richard's Crawfish Patio in Abbeville were among the first to regularly feature crawfish on their menu. The Rainbow Inn of Pierre Part and Al Scramuzza's Seafood City in New Orleans, famous in verse, rhyme and television commercials, also played a major role in expanding the crawfish market. Piccadilly Cafeteria, the famous southern chain, must also be given credit for spreading the gospel of crawfish. Piccadilly began serving crawfish on its Baton Rouge line as early as the mid-1950s[42] and quickly exported the recipe to Lafayette, Lake Charles, Alexandria, New Orleans and Shreveport.

THE RESEARCHERS

Though the Atchafalaya could be an incredible source of crawfish, it was always feast or famine. Some years the basin produced 49 million pounds of crawfish, while the following year's production could be fewer than 2 million pounds. The LSU AgCenter saw the beginnings of its aquaculture research program in 1966,[43] but pioneering researchers like Percy Viosca Jr. paved the way for D.L. Gary, J.B. Dauenhauer, G.H. Penn, Carl Thomas, James Nelson Gowanloch, Cecil LaCaze, Jim Avault, Robert Romaire, Don Gooch, Jay Huner, Jim Fowler and Lawrence (Larry) W. de la Bretonne Jr.

Interstate 10

When Interstate 10's last Acadian section of cement was poured in 1973, President Dwight Eisenhower's dream of a superhighway connecting America and a crawfish in every pot came to fruition. Urban dwellers from Baton Rouge and parts east could suddenly make the drive across the picturesque Atchafalaya Basin in less than an hour to the crawfish restaurants of Henderson. The town's weekday population of nine hundred was tripled by crawfish seekers, who filled three thousand restaurant seats on Friday night.

The Intangibles

Low rice prices, the Great Louisiana Oil Bust, *Le Grande Derangement II*, the great 1980s marketing effort and other intangibles also played pivotal roles in the evolution of the Louisiana crawfish industry. It turned out the gold wasn't necessarily in "them thar hills." It was in the crawfish sacks.

At seventy years old, Mayor Jack Delhomme holds court over Breaux Bridge just like he did in 1958, when he was an All-State track athlete in high school. He still has a great smile, and he moves with a quiet confidence. He stayed late on a Friday in his mayor's office for the first time in years simply because I wanted to talk about the Crawfish Festival.

In Breaux Bridge, crawfish is a subject on which everyone is an expert. "All you had in those days [the '50s] were these fishermen from Henderson who drove through the streets of Breaux Bridge on Friday honking their horns," he said. "You'd come to meet them at the edge of the yard because you couldn't eat meat on Friday."[44] Delhomme spoke emphatically—not like a preacher, but rather a stern-eyed priest trying to ignore Mardi Gras. And as he rose up from his mayor's chair, his voice got louder as he warmed up to the subject. "Who came up with the thought? You buy your crawfish from a fisherman from Henderson because Catholics don't eat meat on Friday, and the next thing you know, we're celebrating one hundred years of Breaux Bridge and Breaux Bridge is the crawfish capital of the world."[45]

"When it comes to crawfish, I'm spoiled. When my grandmother Mathilde Brasseaux Amy cooked her dark-gravy crawfish stew, the tail meat had been peeled by 10:00 a.m. and the stew was ready for dinner [which is what Cajuns call the noon meal in south Louisiana]. MaMa could not read or write, and French was her native tongue. She didn't learn rudimentary English until after her five grandchildren were born. She was your basic rice-and-gravy cook."

MATHILDE BRASSEAUX AMY'S CRAWFISH STEW

2 pounds Louisiana crawfish tail meat

2 heaping tablespoons of roux (*Don't be alarmed—MaMa spent years of her life at the stove stirring roux, and when the first jarred roux became available, she couldn't detect any difference or taste in her stew. If roux in a jar was good enough for MaMa, it's good enough for me.*)

2 large onions

1 green bell pepper

2 garlic pods

2 celery stalks

2 pints water

Warm water on stove, add chopped vegetables and gradually add roux until mixed in well. Bring to a low boil and let the mixture cook down until almost nice and thick. Add crawfish and bring back to a low boil. Let simmer for twenty minutes while seasoning to taste with salt, black pepper and cayenne pepper. Gravy should be dark brown and hearty. Serve over white rice.

CHAPTER 2

WHEN LIFE GIVES YOU CRAWFISH, MAKE ÉTOUFFÉE

In the beginning, there were crawfish, and God said they were good.
Nearly 200 million years later, the Cajuns of south Louisiana added a little salt and cayenne to a simmering pot of crawfish étouffée and agreed with God—crawfish *are* good.

The Native Americans (the Chitimachas, Houmas, Choctaws and Attakapas) of the Mississippi, Teche and Lafourche River Valleys lived in Louisiana when the Spanish arrived in 1528. The French showed up in 1682 and were subsequently followed by the Acadians, English, Germans, Americans, Italians, Croatians, Vietnamese and almost every ethnic group in between. The West Africans didn't have a choice, but they also came.

The crawfish were always here. Every culture that has settled in south Louisiana has fallen in love with the tiny crustacean from the Jurassic Period. In most parts of the United States, the crawfish is used as fish bait and often considered a nuisance.[46] In certain eras, the hardy creature was even considered a pest in Louisiana. "Death to Crawfish" was the column header of a 1904 *St. Tammany Farmer* issue reporting that the levee board was using carbolic acid "with good results to preserve the levees from attack by that clawing and insidious member, the crawfish."[47]

Flood protection levees are important to Louisiana, but so is the crawfish. Some Louisiana Frenchmen believe that the bald eagle should be replaced by the crawfish as the symbol of America. Cajun radio host Revon Reed documented those sentiments in *Lâche Pas la Patate* when he wrote, "We shouldn't make the eagle the symbol of America, but the crawfish. The

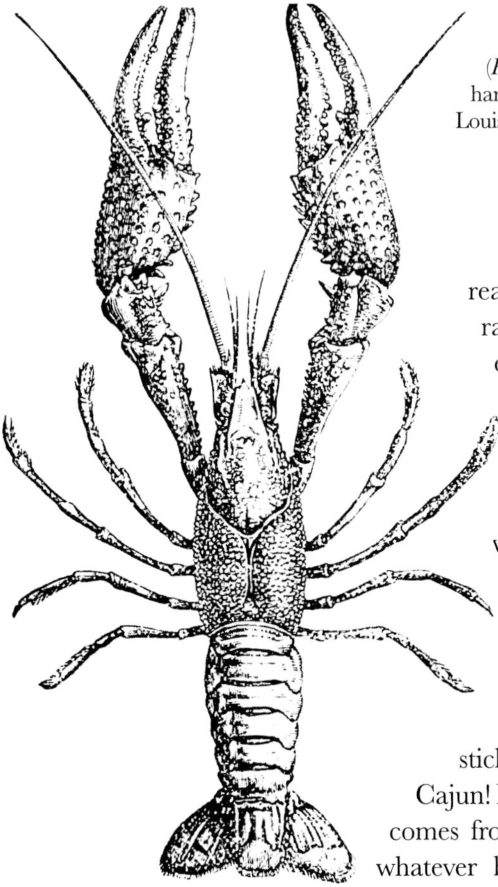

The red swamp crawfish (*Procambarus clarkii*) and white river crawfish (*Procambarus zonangulus*) are the species harvested in the wild and on farms in Louisiana. Pictured here is *P. clarkii*.

reason is simple: put an eagle on a railroad track and what does the eagle do? When a train comes, it raises its wings and flies away. But place *l'écrevisse* on the same rail and when the big locomotive is coming, what will he do? The crawfish raises its claws and will not leave his post! Yes, my friends, that is the crawfish."[48]

Some south Louisiana pickup trucks sport bumper stickers proudly proclaiming, "I'm Cajun! I eat anything!" This declaration comes from a Cajun's propensity to eat whatever he or she can trap, catch or shoot. Like Louisiana pioneers, modern inhabitants will eat squirrel, deer, possum, alligator, frog legs, raccoon, gaspergou, sac-a-lait, boudin (a rice-and-pork sausage), chaudin (pig stomach stuffed with ground pork and seasoning) and mirliton. And it was the lowborn and mostly French-speaking swamp dweller of the Atchafalaya River who taught Louisiana and the world to eat and enjoy crawfish. You could say Cajuns perfected crawfish.

Multiethnic swamp settlers probably learned to eat crawfish from the Native Americans. Incidentally, the Attakapas outdid the omnivorous Cajuns if their reputation as cannibals is deserved—they actually did eat everything.[49]

Eating crawfish is nothing new. Ancient cultures ate crawfish. Sophisticated cultures ate crawfish. Heathens ate crawfish. For Christ's sake, even Queen Elizabeth Tudor, the "Virgin Queen," ate crawfish.[50] But even though Elizabeth tasted crawfish, the crawfish never took hold in England as it did on the European continent. The French and other countries developed an epicurean love of the crawfish.[51] The French developed the complicated and incredibly delicious bisque recipe,[52] while the Swedes' ritualized consumption of crawfish, called *kräftskiva*, reached mythic heights.[53] And the Finns can sit and eat crawfish for "hours."[54] The Europeans even called their native species the "noble crawfish" (*Asticus asticus*). The French and Cajuns who settled in south Louisiana brought an Old World custom of eating crawfish with them, while the English settlers of north Louisiana had no tradition of crawfish consumption at all.[55]

The beginnings of Louisiana's modern crawfish industry roughly coincide with the arrival of the American oilman. Both industries are closely tied to Louisiana's image, and Reed's prediction came true: crawfish did emerge as the prevalent symbol of Cajunism and Louisiana.[56]

The residents of the oil patch initially did not recognize the crawfish as a desirable food source. The oilmen called the crawfish mudbugs, crawdads and yabbies. They called the bilingual Cajuns worse, but the crawfish eventually conquered the oil-field redneck as it did all the other ethnic groups that immigrated to Louisiana.[57]

It is often said that crawfish was once considered a poor man's food and eaten only in the privacy of one's home. The popular myth is not borne out by historical evidence. Some authors have even claimed that "[1927 flood relief] workers from the Red Cross tried to convince Cajuns to eat more crawfish, a widely available and healthy source of protein, but they were generally rebuffed. Crawfish were suitable for eating only during Lent, on Friday (if you couldn't afford fish), and perhaps if starvation were your only alternative. There simply is no long tradition of Cajuns feasting on crawfish on a regular basis in Louisiana."[58]

The reality is that Cajuns were eating and enjoying crawfish prior to the maturing of the 1960s crawfish business, regardless of the religious season. They ate crawfish when crawfish was in season and because they enjoyed the social aspect of the crawfish boil. Some dishes were even considered haute cuisine and served in the finest New Orleans restaurants, as well as in small-town hotels and cafés. But mostly they ate crawfish because crawfish taste good.

Lent does partly coincide with the crawfish season, but the Crescent City residents and Cajuns in Breaux Bridge, Henderson, Catahoula, Arnaudville, Pierre Part, Baton Rouge, Morgan City, St. Martinville, Thibodaux, Abbeville, Lafayette, St. Tammany Parish and dozens of other communities near swampy waterways, ponds and the Atchafalaya Basin[59] fished and ate crawfish when the weather began warming in February, and they had been doing so for years.[60] No media report of the time dispels that fact.

St. Martinville's *Weekly Messenger* reported that the abundant spring rainfall of 1900 "meant a chance for the [St. Martin Parish] swampers and a large crawfish crop."[61] In 1906, the St. Martinville Town Council allowed crawfish sales within town limits only at the public market house[62] and later set the cost of a "stall for the sale of crawfish at fifty cents per day" in 1918.[63]

The *Weekly Messenger* also admonished businessmen with know-how in 1915 to look into canning facilities because "our bayous and lakes [produce] immense quantities of fish and shell fish, buffalo, cat, bass, perch, crabs, crawfish [and] turtle."[64]

In Donaldsonville, on Bayou Lafourche, the June 25, 1921 *Chief* reported, "River shrimp and crawfish are very plentiful this year, and are sold at prices lower than those which prevailed last year. Crawfish can be bought at 25 cents the bucket. Farm hands on the rice plantations are regaling themselves with the delicious and nourishing crawfish, while colored children are earning extra money selling them to the white folks in town."[65]

In Opelousas, the 1919 Knights of Columbus "gave a delicious crayfish gumbo at the order's home on Main Street. The gumbo was of the real 'Louisiana kind' and was thoroughly enjoyed by the many who were present for the occasion."[66]

Floyd Knott, seventy-nine, of Arnaudville said the resourceful rural dwellers of the 1930s could catch their own crawfish quite easily:

> *During Lent, there was usually a plentiful supply of crawfish. After a rain, the ditches became muddy with them. Some people still believe that the crawfish were attracted to the mud, but that was not true. Crawfish prefer clean water; it is just that they were so plentiful that in an effort to scratch for food the water became muddy. But the muddy water indicated that crawfish were to be caught, and the only way that they were caught in the '30s and '40s was with a pole net which we called a* carrelet.[67]

There are dozens of mentions in the society pages of crawfishing as a social activity as well.

"A party composed of Misses May and Elmira Frost and Laura Lagarde, Messrs. Gus Wallace Fulton Rogers and Henry Bergeron enjoyed a delightful outing on Leighton Plantation during the week. Crawfishing was the pastime, and the catch made was excellent," the *Weekly Thibodaux Sentinel* of April 27, 1901, noted.

Richard's Crawfish Patio in Abbeville, Louisiana, a rice country town, began featuring boiled crawfish as early as 1952. *Sam Irwin.*

In turn-of-the-nineteenth-century Lafayette, "Mr. and Mrs. S. J. Breaux entertained at a social dinner last Sunday. Dinner was served *à la française* as follows: red and white wines, red fish, quail, teal duck, crawfish salad with aspic."[68]

The *Beaumont Enterprise*'s March 17, 1935 banner headline, "Tasty Crawfish Dishes Add to Teche Culinary Fame," reported that Mr. and Mrs. Pee Wee Gagnon of Abbeville had been known for crawfish dishes in their eatery for years. Dean Tevis, the feature's writer, even put President Hebert Hoover at the table of the Hebert Hotel in Breaux Bridge as he dined on "Mother Hebert's crawfish bisque."[69] Tevis said that "a jaunt of a hundred and fifty miles from Texas for crawfish bisque is rather commonplace" and that "in the rural sections of the territory, crawfishing from two to four months every year is one of the chief occupations and certainly the leading pastime of its picturesque people."[70]

The March 20, 1932 *Times-Picayune* dedicated more than half a page to a feature called "Fearless Little Crawfish Supplies Wayside Industry and Affords Family Sport" and the sub-headline of "Ditches Along Main Roads Teem with Crustaceans Rich in Food Value and Waiting to Be Caught by Professional Fishermen or Amateur." Reporter Podine Schoenberger wrote, "Marshland dwellers are trappers one season, moss-pickers and crabbers the next, and the fishermen find crawfishing the easiest job of them all."[71]

In *Catholic Life in Rural Louisiana*, Reverend Herman Joseph Jacobi wrote the following of the 1937 Pierre Part community of Assumption Parish: "During the summer there is an abundance of crabs, and in the spring, of crawfish. For the families, this [crawfish] is just another variety of fish."[72] Jacobi mentions a 1932 Pierre Part crawfish-peeling operation that canned crawfish bisque for resale for area markets being in operation for at least three years before it turned a profit in 1936.[73]

There were other crawfishing canning plants in the Atchafalaya and Mississippi River flood plains. The Forêt family of LaPlace, just twenty miles east of New Orleans, processed crawfish caught by the Forêt children and area residents in the 1930s. That the crawfish were harvested with simple lift nets is an indication of how abundant the fisheries just west of New Orleans were. New Orleans buyers traveled to LaPlace to buy the live product, and the Forêts peeled the remaining crawfish to can crawfish bisque.[74]

Odas Dugas of Coteau Holmes owned a dump truck that was used to build the West Atchafalaya Basin Protection levee. A commercial fisherman, he also caught large quantities of crawfish in the spring. The Coteau Holmes area was not a very large population center, so to market his crawfish in the late 1940s, Dugas would leave sacks of crawfish at the end of the road near his boat launch. Customers would drive to the location and leave money for the crawfish. Eventually, Dugas began to deliver his crawfish to the Lafayette–Breaux Bridge area, and one of his customers was Edwin "Mulate" Guidry of Mulate's Restaurant and Bar in Breaux Bridge. A steady supply of crawfish guaranteed, Mulate's began to sell crawfish dishes on a regular basis.[75]

Breaux Bridge and St. Martin Parish had become so well known for the production of écrevisse that the well-to-do state representative Bob Angelle of Breaux Bridge referred to himself in 1946 as "a little old country boy from the crawfish country."[76]

Floyd Knott says there was no class distinction associated with crawfish consumption. Rural or city resident, rich or poor, people ate crawfish in season because the crustaceans were there for the taking. "We never considered ourselves *basse classe* [low class], only rural folks who made the best use of our resources. If city folks could have gotten the crawfish, I am sure that they would have savored the dish. No restaurant featured the dishes mostly because there were no restaurants in the country and rural folks seldom went to the big cities," he surmised.[77]

City folks did get crawfish, however, and the feasts prepared were considered exclusive and celebratory treats.

The 1915 version of the Baton Rouge Elks Club was putting the finishing touches on "the Eatmore club [and] will resume their periodical Bohemian luncheons, varying the events as the seasons change. Crawfish bisque will be the principal attraction at the first of these, to be held within a fortnight; then as shrimp and fish come in season, they will be featured. When it comes to real enjoyment, without frills or furbelows, the Elks stand in a class by themselves."[78]

Perhaps the only shame associated with crawfish is to be guilty of not seasoning the food well enough. The overwhelming evidence indicates that crawfish was a seasonal delicacy and a celebrated attraction for any social group or function. In other words, when life gives you crawfish, make étouffée.

Nevertheless, the myth that crawfish was once a poor man's food and not to be eaten in polite company remains. Perhaps the origin of that fable arrived with the oilman. There were some, perhaps wishing to avoid being called "backwards" by the nouveau riche oilmen, who would not eat crawfish in public lest they be associated with uneducated swamp dwellers.

"I think the stigma associated with crawfish popped up just about the time the oil industry arrived in Louisiana," said Dickie Breaux, owner of the popular Café des Amis in downtown Breaux Bridge. "The only place the oil field workers ever saw crawfish was in the sewage pond. They didn't relate to the clean-water crawfish that grew in the Atchafalaya Basin and rice fields."[79]

Ironically, today's crawfish market is partly driven by the big oil cities, as well as the other southern metro areas. "The crawfish demand is worldwide, but now there's a great demand in major cities like Houston, Dallas, Atlanta and New Orleans," said Ashby "Rocky" Landry Jr., owner of Don's Seafood and Steakhouse in Lafayette. "And they don't care about the price. They will pay seven or eight dollars a pound [for a catered party] if the crawfish are purged and big. And if you tell them that's the price, they'll say, 'So what?'"

If you're a middle-class Cajun who likes to have crawfish regularly, *ça c'est triste* (that's a tragedy), but if you're a crawfish merchant, *ça c'est bien bon* (that's real good).

Fortunately, Cajun self-esteem has risen over time. Any perceived stigma is in the past. In the 2012–13 season, Louisiana produced more than 93 million pounds of crawfish in just twenty-nine parishes[80] (284 square miles)—an area a little larger than the island nation of St. Kitts and Nevis.

How did the lowly Louisiana crawfish, a so-called poor man's food, emerge from the muck and become the state crustacean, the symbol of a culture and a valuable aquaculture worth $162 million a year?[81]

CRAWFISH BISQUE

Before the days of the commercial crawfish-peeling facility, if you wanted to impress someone, you served him crawfish bisque. Preparing the bisque, meaning "twice-cooked," entailed scalding live crawfish, peeling them and then stuffing each individual head with bisque. The dish is totally worth it. Here is Don's Seafood and Steakhouse of Lafayette's recipe for bisque served in stew.

CRAWFISH BISQUE HEADS

20 pounds crawfish or 3 pounds tail meat
1 cup celery, chopped
2 cups onions, chopped
½ pound oleo
½ cup green onions and parsley, chopped
4 eggs
3 stale buns, soaked in water, salt and cayenne (red pepper) to taste
1 cup breadcrumbs

Scald the crawfish. Put enough water in a heavy pot so that the crawfish will be covered with four inches of water and then bring to a boil. Drop the crawfish into the boiling water and then immediately turn off the heat. Let the crawfish set uncovered in hot water for five minutes. Drain the water and then peel the crawfish, saving the fat. After scalding the crawfish, separate the tails from the heads. Inside the crawfish head is a yellow substance—this is the "fat." Remove this fat from all of the crawfish heads and then set aside with crawfish tails and head. Combine oleo, onions and celery in heavy iron pot and let cook uncovered over medium heat until onions are wilted, stirring constantly. Add crawfish fat and cook slowly for fifteen minutes. Season to taste with salt, black pepper and cayenne. Add soaked buns and mix well with eggs and breadcrumbs. Chop half the scalded crawfish tails. Add chopped tails, green onions and parsley to cooked mixture. Stuff crawfish heads with the mixture and serve with crawfish stew made with the remaining crawfish tails. Serve the stew with cooked white rice in soup bowls with about five stuffed heads in each bowl. Serves eight.

CRAWFISH STEW

1½ pounds crawfish tail meat
2 cups onions, chopped
1 cup celery, chopped
½ can whole tomatoes
4 cloves garlic, minced
1 level teaspoon tomato paste
1 cup all-purpose flour
1 cup cooking oil
½ cup green onions and parsley, chopped
1 gallon cold water
Salt, pepper and cayenne (red pepper)

To make a roux, put oil in heavy iron pot over medium heat. When oil is hot, gradually stir in flour and then lower heat. It is very important to stir constantly. After all of the flour and oil is combined, lower heat and cook until golden brown. After the roux becomes desired color, remove from pot and place into another container until ready for use. (Roux will become too dark if left in warm pot.) (Editor's note: in lieu of cooking roux, you may substitute four heaping tablespoons of pre-cooked jarred roux.) Add onions, celery, whole tomatoes and tomato paste to roux. Cook in heavy uncovered pot over medium heat for about forty minutes or until oil separates from tomatoes. Set aside. Put one gallon of water, garlic and the crawfish fat in uncovered pot over medium heat, stirring constantly until boiling. Season generously with salt, black pepper and cayenne. Add roux mixture. Cook in uncovered pot for one hour. Add crawfish tails and continue boiling slowly in uncovered pot for another twenty minutes. Add green onions and parsley. Serve in soup plates with cooked rice and stuffed bisque heads.

CHAPTER 3

THE CRAWFISH CAPITAL OF THE WORLD

Catching the crawfish, peeling the tail meat and filling crawfish heads with bisque stuffing is quite labor intensive. There's no doubt that Cajuns and Creoles were enjoying crawfish, but it takes a lot of work to put a crawfish recipe on the table and serve it on a regular basis. That may be the reason the crawfish business was slow to mature. To make an étouffée for four diners, thirty pounds of crawfish must be peeled; for a party of fifteen, one has to go through two hundred pounds of live crawfish—no easy task.[82]

Louisiana Department of Wildlife and Fisheries chief biologist James Nelson Gowanloch summed up the problem: "Virtually everyone in Louisiana knows much about crayfish even though many, like the writer, are too lazy to eat them unless some patient person has prepared them in the much more easily enjoyed form of crayfish bisque."[83] However, someone was peeling, packing and canning crawfish because Gowanloch indicated in his 1951 report that "crayfish for dinner to those unenlightened Americans who live in abandoned ignorance in such northern fastnesses as Minnesota and Wisconsin means merely the juxtaposition of one can opener and one can of (preferably from Louisiana) crayfish bisque."[84]

As previously cited, entrepreneurs were peeling crawfish and canning crawfish bisque in Pierre Part as early as 1932[85] and in LaPlace in the 1930s.[86]

Gourmets were hopping trains from Texas and Lafayette to sample crawfish at Breaux Bridge's Hebert Hotel and Guittreaux's in the 1920s and the Gagnon lunchroom in Abbeville in the 1930s because they tasted so good.

Essie Dupuis of Breaux Bridge (white shirt in back) watches as peelers collect the tail meat and fat from par-boiled crawfish in 1959. *Ashton Roberthon family.*

Someone was organizing a labor force and peeling crawfish.[87] The gold must be in those crawfish holes somewhere. All it was going to take was a little promotion and entrepreneurship. The promotion was provided by the town of Breaux Bridge, and the entrepreneurship came from Abby Latiolais, Joe Amy, Berthmonse Montet, Aristile Robin,[88] Freddy Zerangue,[89] Harris and Aline Champagne, Pat and Agnes Huval, Mulate Guidry and Don Landry.

The promotion of the crawfish began with a simple letter written by Lafayette judge A. Wilmot Dalferes to Breaux Bridge resident Anna Belle Dupuis Hoffman in 1958. Judge Dalferes liked to rummage through dusty old courthouse records, and in the spring of 1958, he discovered that Breaux Bridge was due for a birthday, the centennial anniversary of the town's incorporation.[90] Breaux Bridge historian Grover Rees harrumphed that the town was actually founded much earlier when Firmin Breaux built a suspended footbridge over the Bayou Teche in 1799, but Dalferes wasn't concerned about the founding.[91] He had a document in hand that detailed the town's incorporation. He wrote a letter to Anna Belle, a teacher "active in more things (school, civic and social) in Breaux Bridge than there are ways of preparing crayfish."[92] Anna Belle brought the news to her boss at the St. Martin Parish School Board, Assistant Superintendent Raymond Castille.

In 1959, Anna Belle Hoffman (pictured here serenading Woody Marshall and a crawfish dog) proposed celebrating Breaux Bridge's 100th anniversary by honoring the crawfish. *Ashton Roberthon family.*

Castille said he brought the information to the Lion's Club, but it seems like Anna Belle did all the heavy lifting. If anyone could convince the local Lions to spend months planning a celebration that would bring an estimated thirty to seventy thousand visitors to their sleepy bayou town, that person was Anna Belle. Educated, vivacious and with an infectious, toothy smile, Anna Belle could, by sheer force of character, sell sand to Saharans.

Technically, the town was incorporated on March 14, but that was smack in the middle of Lent.[93] Catholics in Breaux Bridge penanced not only on Lenten Fridays but also Wednesdays. They recited the Rosary every night, and many attended daily Mass. A centennial celebration during Quadragesima just wouldn't do.[94] Anna Belle and the Lions settled on the second weekend in April. With the Lion's Club on board, Castille convinced Mayor Louis Kern and the town council to back a centennial celebration. The deciding factor was probably that it would be funded completely with self-generated monies.

In a stunning act of public relations brilliance, centennial organizers chose the crawfish as the symbol of the city and persuaded Governor Earl K. Long and the Louisiana legislature to declare Breaux Bridge the *Capitale Mondiale de l'Écrevisse* (Crawfish Capital of the World). Robert "Bob" Angelle, Breaux Bridge's elected state representative and Long's handpicked Speaker of the House, shepherded the resolution through the legislature.

Why the crawfish? What claim did Breaux Bridge have to the kingdom of crawfish? There was ample precedent.

Newspaper articles from the 1920s and '30s cite St. Martin Parish and Breaux Bridge specifically as a crawfish center. The May 12, 1928 *State-Times* reported that the coaches and officials from Centenary, Louisiana College, Louisiana Normal, Louisiana Tech, Mississippi College, Ogelthorpe and Presbyterian attending the Southern Intercollegiate Athletic Association track meet at Lafayette's Southwestern Louisiana Institute were "guests at a crayfish supper last night at the Hebert Hotel in Breaux Bridge."[95]

Morning Advocate food reporter Nita Sims Breazeale advised her May 14, 1935 readers that there were many "unique places to eat…up the rivers and down the bayous of Louisiana." She mentioned Breaux Bridge's Hebert's Hotel "for the feast of the crayfish—a dinner of crayfish cocktail, crayfish salad, crayfish pie, crayfish stew, crayfish patties, crayfish soup gumbo and bisque l'ecrivisse [*sic*]. Guittreaux's, there, has very good food too."[96]

The *Beaumont Enterprise* noted that Herbert Hoover had dined on crawfish at the Hebert Hotel and that day trips via rail to feast on crawfish were not uncommon.[97] Breaux Bridge was also singled out for its crawfish cuisine when Hollywood actress Dolores Del Rio starred in *Evangeline*, a 1929 movie about the deportation and subsequent resettlement of Canada's French Acadians (Louisiana's future Cajuns) in south Louisiana. Del Rio donated a bronze statue of Evangeline, the fictional character made famous by Henry Wadsworth Longfellow's epic poem, to St. Martinville in 1932. The unveiling, Louisiana's version of a Hollywood movie premier, was organized by popular Louisiana politician and creator of the famous Hadacol tonic, Dudley "Coozan Dud" J. Leblanc. Thousands attended the ceremony as Leblanc led a group of visiting French Canadian dignitaries on a tour of the Bayou Teche Valley that included a parade through downtown Breaux Bridge. The visit to the future crawfish capital of the world was highlighted by "a crawfish bisque supper, a famed Creole dish in south Louisiana [that] was served to nearly 500 persons under the 'paradise oaks' located on the west banks of the Teche."[98]

Breaux Bridge, now nicknamed the "Gabriel City"[99] in honor of Evangeline's much-suffering beau, had firmly established a reputation as a crawfish city. A librarian's convention in New Orleans made its way to bayou country, and "the historic Evangeline oak was visited…and a real Creole dinner—the 12 o'clock kind—was served at Breaux Bridge. It was there that many of the visiting librarians got their first taste of that well-known Louisiana dish, crayfish bisque."[100]

New Orleans mayor deLesseps "Chep" Morrison referred to Breaux Bridge as the "Crawfish Capital" in a 1955 economic development speech that he delivered in French to Breaux Bridge residents. Morrison was said to be the "kind of mayor who looks right taking Zsa Zsa Gabor to tea." [101] A man that debonair obviously knows something about cuisine.

"Sing, Goddess of the noble mudbug!" wrote the *Times-Picayune*'s Pie Dufour in his April 3, 1955 "A La Mode" column.[102] When the society columnist of the state's leading newspaper writes heroic verse about the crawfish dishes of Breaux Bridge, something classic is going on. Dufour continued his love letter to Breaux Bridge's crawfish as he rewrote poet Robert Browning in the same column: "O, to be in Breaux Bridge, now that crawfish are there!" Two years later, the genteel Mrs. Max Schenker of Baton Rouge's *State-Times* repeated the same Browning-inspired quote in her April 4 column with one difference—she offered hope to those who could not be in Breaux Bridge. "It's not necessary to be in southwest Louisiana. You can have your crawfish and eat it here," she counseled. All one had to do was follow a marvelous sounding crawfish pie recipe that she shared in the column.

INDIVIDUAL CRAWFISH PIES

3 tablespoons butter
3 tablespoons flour
1 teaspoon chopped celery top
1 teaspoon chopped parsley

1 teaspoon chopped green onion

1¾ cup water

Scalded, picked crawfish tails

Salt and pepper to taste

Brown the flour and onion in the butter, add water and stir until smooth. Add other seasoning. Add the tails of the crawfish, using enough for a generous serving for each. Use small, thinly rolled pie crust. The crust may be used only on top if desired. Fill dishes quite full of the mixture and cover with dough rolled thinly and pricked well with a fork. Bake in a hot oven for fifteen minutes or thirty minutes in a moderate oven if under crust is used.

(Recipe from the Louisiana Department of Conservation bulletin *Fishes and Fishing in Louisiana*.)[103]

But talk about crawfish world hegemony induced stuffy Howard Jacobs, another *Times-Picayune* society writer, to sniff about the proliferation of "world capitals" in his "Remoulade" column. "We've always fatuously assumed that Louisiana had but one capital," Jacobs huffed. "But we were speedily undeceived on finding in the myriad of ads by cities and towns that the state contains more world capitals than the law allows. Rayne is assertedly the 'frog capital of the world,' Breaux Bridge is 'crawfish capital of the world' and Hammond is 'strawberry capital of the world.' Bogalusa modestly confined itself to the state in pre-empting the title 'pine tree capital of Louisiana.'"[104]

Nonetheless, Jacobs acknowledged that Breaux Bridge was forever the crawfish capital.

Heroic verse, a speech made in French by a man handsome enough to escort Zsa Zsa and a state-issued tourist guide declaring the sleepy bayou town as the crawfish capital? Who could deny Breaux Bridge's newfound status?

Well, other crawfish-producing towns.

Henderson restaurateur and former mayor Pat Huval said that he ceded the crawfish capital claim to Breaux Bridge because it was a town with a downtown.[105] *Morning Advocate* sportswriter Bob Scearce, disagreeing with Mayor Chep and Mayor Huval, wrote, "In the crawfish capital of the world, Pierre Part, the mudbugs are coming in in more abundant quantities."[106]

Commemorative Centennial license plates were sold for two dollars to help generate funding for Breaux Bridge's Centennial Celebration. The celebration evolved into the Crawfish Festival. *Ashton Roberthon family.*

Les Braves Barbes of Breaux Bridge and Louisiana Speaker of the House Bob Angelle ensure passage of the Crawfish Capital resolution at the state capitol in 1959. *Ashton Roberthon family.*

Alas, though Pierre Part was a crawfish fiefdom in its own right, it did not have a Bob Angelle, a Speaker of the House or a concurrent resolution signed by a mad governor.

Café des Amis owner Dickie Breaux was a former Louisiana state representative for the Jeanerette, Iberia Parish area in 1968. Breaux,

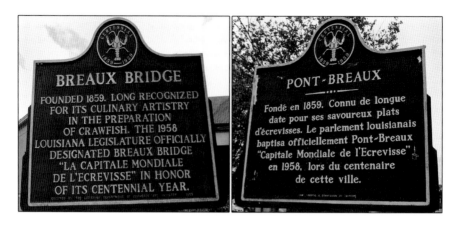

Breaux Bridge's bilingual historic marker incorrectly cites the town's founding as 1859. The town's first bridge was built in 1799, and Breaux Bridge was actually founded in 1829 and incorporated in 1859. *Sam Irwin.*

a Breaux Bridge native, said he took a lot of ribbing from Pierre Part politicians who discounted Breaux Bridge's daring claim to the crawfish pie. Breaux deftly quieted his Pierre Part counterparts from Assumption Parish with this rejoinder: "Did any of you invite the rest of the nation to visit Louisiana to honor the crawfish? The answer was no, and that shut them up."[107]

Long, aka the "Last of the Red Hot Pappas," and the state legislature merely rubber-stamped what anyone who was anyone already knew: if you wanted to eat the best crawfish, you came to Breaux Bridge.[108]

So why did the Louisiana legislature, which was not generally known as a progressive body, recognize Breaux Bridge's "culinary artistry in the preparation of crawfish"? Because it was true.

Obviously, something good was cooking in the kitchens of Breaux Bridge, and crawfish were well known in the dining halls of the Hebert Hotel and Guittreaux's in the 1920s.[109]

Mrs. Charles Hebert (pronounced *A-bear*), proprietress of the Hebert Hotel, is generally credited as being the first to serve crawfish étouffée, though she called it a courtbouillon. Her Main Street establishment in Breaux Bridge was known near and far as the best place to dine on crawfish,[110] and it attracted gastronomes who traveled by train to sample her recipes.[111]

The recipe faded away, Breaux said, because "Mrs. Hebert's daughters, Yolie and Marie, had problems and their hotel closed." The dish apparently lay in limbo until Mrs. Hebert's daughters passed the recipe on to Aline

Guidry Champagne, who resurrected it by accident at the Rendezvous Club in the late '40s.[112]

The Rendezvous Club and Restaurant (1948–53) was located on Grand Pointe Road not far from the La Poussiere Dance Hall in Breaux Bridge. "We always ate crawfish during the fishing season, especially during Lent, when few people ate meat," Aline said. "I remember, though, that I didn't care for crawfish the way most people prepared it—too spicy."[113]

Aline didn't want to overpower the flavor of the crawfish with garlic and celery. "I always fixed my own crawfish plates," she said. "I cooked the crawfish fat with a little cooking oil, parsley, onion tops and onions and then heated the crawfish tails in the pot. I didn't serve crawfish to our customers that way, though. They seemed to prefer the traditional stews and bisque or crawfish patties. But one night I was eating my own dinner when Mr. and Mrs. Martin Begnaud came in, so I offered them a plate. Then a group of people I knew from Lafayette came in to the restaurant for supper and ordered whatever we were eating. And that's how it all started."[114]

Breaux reported that Begnaud, the president of Farmers & Merchants Bank, returned the next Friday with his employees and ordered crawfish étouffée.[115] Possibly uncertain of how to spell étouffée, the dish appeared on the menu as "Crayfish E'tau-fait" in English and "Écrevisse Étouffée" in French. It cost $1.50 a plate in 1950.[116]

A faded circa 1966 typewritten press release from the Breaux Bridge Crawfish Festival Association recounts a similar story about Aline, the Rendezvous and crawfish étouffée:

> *One night in 1949 after a very tiring workday, Aileen [sic] decided to fix herself some crawfish, but she didn't feel like eating stew or bisque, so she cooked up something that was delicious. Some friends, Martin and Doris Begnaud, were there and saw it and tasted it. Mon Aimee, delicious. "Why don't you sell this, Aileen [sic]? What is it?" Nobody had ever served this particular dish before. So they all put their heads together and decided to call it "étouffée." This has become the queen of all the crawfish dishes. And it happened here in Breaux Bridge.[117]*

The *Teche News* article does concede that there may be an argument over whether Aline actually created the dish or simply originated the étouffée name, but no one disputes that she and her husband operated the first crawfish-peeling plant in Breaux Bridge in the 1950s, with twelve to fifteen women hired as peelers to supply the fresh tail meat needed by the restaurant.[118]

Mulate Guidry was one of the early Breaux Bridge marketers of crawfish and began buying and peeling crawfish in the early 1950s. His brother was Henderson founder Henry Guidry. *Breaux Bridge Crawfish Festival Association.*

It's significant that Aline's father was Henderson founder and restaurateur/dancehall operator Henry Guidry and her uncle Edwin "Mulate" Guidry, an early crawfish merchant in Breaux Bridge who dealt in peeled and live crawfish. Mulate Guidry also hired Gladys Breaux, the unparalleled crawfish chef of Breaux Bridge. Gladys peeled crawfish at her house and prepared many a crawfish meal for catered parties at the Breaux Bridge Veterans Home.[119] The Guidry trio is very important to the development of the modern crawfish industry.

Henry Guidry's Henderson restaurant evolved into the crawfish-specializing Pat's Fisherman's Wharf Restaurant, which is still in operation and sporting a heavily air-conditioned dance hall. Mulate Guidry created Mulate's Restaurant. A branch of Mulate's is still in operation in New Orleans, but the original Mulate's location in Breaux Bridge suffered extensive damage during Hurricane Gustav in 2008 and is now known as Pont Breaux's.

Ultimately, the Hebert/Guidry Champagne étouffée has become the "queen" dish of the crawfish cookbook. It's easier and much less time-consuming to prepare than bisque. The recipe is simple: sauté onion in oil, add crawfish with crawfish fat and smother and serve over white rice. Étouffée features the sublime texture of the tail meat and the total umami of the crawfish fat. The so-called fat is actually an organ called the hepatopancreas and functions as the animal's liver, but the fat is the singular ingredient in all crawfish dishes that makes crawfish taste like crawfish. It's the true taste of crawfish, and that is why the best-tasting crawfish is always freshly peeled, never frozen and eaten in season. Nothing else can compare.

However, if Mrs. Charles Hebert and Aline Guidry Champagne had not created and popularized crawfish étouffée, it's very likely that another inventive cook would have.

Breaux Bridge's Centennial Celebration turned out to be the stage debut of the crawfish. Volunteer high school students painted pictures of crawfish on commemorative plaques and sold them to collectors. Local commercial artist Woodrow Marshall designed a souvenir centennial flag, ashtray and bandanna featuring the Cajun crustacean. Crawfish pins were visible on every jacket lapel. The town sold a tabloid-sized souvenir program that included limited editions of the *Centennial News*, and a special automobile license plate could be had for two dollars.[120]

Borrowing gimmicks from centennial celebrations from other Cajun towns, the centennial committee decided that the men would grow beards as a throwback to honor their nineteenth-century forebears. The ladies would dress in what they believed was appropriate period garb accented by old-fashioned *gardes-soleil* (sunbonnets), lace-up boots and long dresses.

Les Braves Barbes (The Gallant Beards) and *Les Belles du Centenaire du Pont Breaux* (The Ladies of the Breaux Bridge Centennial) promoted the old-timey nature of the celebration with the fervor of a good door-to-door salesman. They advertised via radio, TV, newspaper and, most importantly, word of mouth.

Emissaries of Les Braves Barbes visited Port Arthur, Texas, and Les Belles wooed revelers in the nearby Acadian cities of St. Martinville, New Iberia and Lafayette.[121] Les Braves Barbes marched in the Houma Mardi Gras parade and then went on to Baton Rouge, where they received the keys to the city and spread the centennial news. After they conquered Baton Rouge, they visited Mayor Morrison in New Orleans to talk crawfish and walked out with the Crescent City's keys.[122]

Soon, Les Braves Barbes had more than seven hundred members, each of whom had forked over a dollar bill for the right to grow a beard. Men in

The souvenir Breaux Bridge Centennial Celebration program package included a schedule placard and the three editions of the specially published *Centennial News*. *Ashton Roberthon family.*

Men who did not grow their beards to help celebrate Breaux Bridge's centennial celebration were subject to a kangaroo court and fined. *Ashton Roberthon family*.

adjoining communities grew their beards in a show of solidarity. Radio and TV personalities from nearby Lafayette grew their whiskers and publicized the event. At the Breaux Bridge Veterans Home, dances were staged and beards and ladies' old-fashioned dresses judged to raise money and local interest. These soirees were also the setting for kangaroo courts to judge the beardless men who ventured to show up with smooth chins. The penalty for not growing a beard? A cash fine and the forced wearing of a "yellow chicken" lapel pin. All of the money collected went into a fund to help produce the centennial.

Kangaroo court prosecutor Harris Periou swore an oath "by the succulent Crawfish in the Bayou, by all you have caught, eaten or even hope to catch, to defend the honor of *Les Braves Barbes*, to uphold and to defend the sweetness, *Les Belles du Centenaire du Pont Breaux*, and to prosecute to the fullest extent of your power and law every beardless man of legal age who shall live in or invade the borders and confines of our fair Breaux Bridge."[123] Even the exalted Speaker of the House, Bob Angelle, who had been so instrumental in creating the Crawfish Capital mystique, forked over fifty dollars because he remained clean-shaven.

Perhaps because of the apparent novelty of crawfish, the corniness of Les Brave Barbes and Les Belles Centenaire continued to receive a goodly amount of newspaper coverage in the *Teche News*, *Daily Advertiser*, *Times-Picayune*, *Morning Advocate*, *State-Times*, *Port Arthur News* and *Beaumont Enterprise*.

In November 1958, the *Daily Advertiser* listed the dozens of Breaux Bridge residents serving on planning committees, including Raymond Castille, Earl Hollier, Joel Periou, John Allen Breaux, Ralph Leblanc, Anna Belle Hoffman, Woodrow Marshall, Irby Landry, Elsie Castille, Jeanne Castille, Ashton Roberthon, Alberie Degeyter, Mavis Finley, Bill Clause, Louis Kern and Ovey Patin.[124]

"Publicity is everybody's business," said publicity chair Ashton Roberthon. Roberthon urged everyone to "visit the attic of the house, look in the old trunks for photos or old family belongings and perhaps from these old heirlooms will unfold the theme for a heartwarming human interest story appropriate for Centennial Publicity."

Dufour, who had already waxed so eloquently in his "A La Mode" column, hyped the "huge crayfish boil" that was to be staged in the city park, the water heated by a wood fire in the days before one could go to any convenience store and buy a full crawfish boiling set-up.[125]

It's odd that Dufour would refer to the Cajun crustacean as "crayfish" in previewing the 1959 celebration when, a full five years earlier, he had written, "Purists may call 'em crayfish…but in these parts, pardner, those who eat 'em by the bucket load call 'em crawfish."[126]

A word on the crawfish/crayfish debate. "Crawfish" was first used by "eccentric naturalist" Constantine Rafinesque when he was working in the Ohio River basin near Kentucky. The word "crayfish," based on the French word *écrevisse*, was popularized by English biologist T.H. Huxley in his 1880 tome titled *The Crayfish: An Introduction to the Study of Zoology*.[127]

Perhaps Dufour had inherited a new copy editor who believed that if it wasn't in the dictionary, it wasn't a word. The *New York Times* generally prefers to use "crayfish" in its copy, and former managing editor Dale Irvin of Baton Rouge's *Country Roads* magazine said the "Grey Lady" refused to let him use "crawfish" in his *Ten Things You Could Do in New Orleans Before Katrina*.[128]

"If we're talking about regional dishes, we try to explain why we used crawfish instead of crayfish," said Zach Johnk, the *Times*' assistant to the senior editor of standards. "I'm sure there have been plenty of references to 'crawfish' over the years."[129]

Les Braves Barbes present Louisiana governor Earl K. Long with a Breaux Bridge flag. Long signed the documents establishing Breaux Bridge as the Crawfish Capital of the World in 1958. *Ashton Roberthon family*.

The question was obviously settled for *Picayune* reader John M'Closkey of Hammond, who opined in an April 15, 1959 letter to the editor that "a law should be passed requiring everyone in Louisiana to use the name crawfish…[and] not the Yankee term crayfish or crawdad."

The sweet filling in the publicity pie was achieved when Governor Long received Les Braves Barbes in his chamber on March 9, a month before the Centennial *belle affaire*. The *Times-Picayune* capital correspondent hammered up the visit in his story, writing, "Eleven bushy-bearded gentlemen, with dress top-hats, silk vests, and an air of stern efficiency, slipped quietly into the governor's office. [They] could have been taken for early-time steamboat gamblers."[130]

Why was this event so significant? Well, the Louisiana press and more than a few national papers followed every move that ol' Earl Long made, and if Earl was receiving the bearded men from Breaux Bridge, well, heck, that deserved coverage in the *Picayune, Morning Advocate, State-Times* and *Teche News*. That was good news for the Breaux Bridge Centennial Celebration and the crawfish.

In the days before television, following Louisiana politics was a spectator sport. Politicians performed on the state capitol milieu created by Huey Long, where bullet holes from his 1935 assassination had become a tourist attraction. Jimmie Davis, the music and movie star who wrote and sang the hit "You Are My Sunshine," had already won the 1944 governorship once and attracted a lot of national media attention to the state. In a state known for producing flamboyant politicians, what could Earl Long do to make hard-boiled newsmen stand up and take notice? Well, a lot.

Since Long was constitutionally barred from succeeding himself, he outrageously intimated a number of times that he would resign the governorship and allow Lieutenant Governor Lethar Frazar to assume the post. Then ol' Earl would run in the 1959 campaign, win and succeed Frazar in a nifty two-step around state law.[131]

Seemingly, whenever Earl spoke, he created controversy. In a time of segregationists, Earl Long claimed he was the one being segregated. "I'm segregated," he said. "Why there's the [exclusive] Boston Club in New Orleans. If ever I went there, they'd use an insecticide to get me out."[132] He became estranged from his wife, Blanche, after he built her a mansion on "Millionaire's Row"[133] in Baton Rouge. Declaring it too big, he began wooing twenty-three-year-old stripper Blaze Starr, who performed every night at Bourbon Street's Sho-Bar in New Orleans.[134] After sitting at the Sho-Bar every night until 3:30 a.m., he'd have a state trooper drive him back to the Baton Rouge governor's mansion for a bit of sleep. Then he'd rise at 6:30 a.m., pour himself a shot of bourbon and place a bet on every horse race in the country.[135]

Capitol followers had come to expect a certain level of absurdity from its politicians, but they began to suspect something was up when ol' Earl dropped thirty pounds. Capitol correspondent Walt Benton noted, "For the first time in many months, he [Long] is smoking cigarettes again [and] his press conferences are unusually quiet and peaceful."[136] Contemporary accounts chalked all of this up to Earl's normal eccentric behavior, but those closest to Earl knew the governor was newly separated from his wife and "consuming huge quantities of Dexedrine."[137]

Les Braves Barbes didn't know anything about Long's substance abuse; all they wanted was for the governor to come down to Breaux Bridge, eat some crawfish and enjoy Breaux Bridge's hospitality, so they invited him to visit. Long accepted.

Speaker of the House Angelle arranged for a political rally to be added to the centennial, and the stage was set for the biggest event in Breaux Bridge's one-hundred-year incorporated history.

The Catholic Mass procession that opened the 1959 Breaux Bridge Centennial Celebration. The Catholic practice of abstaining from meat on Fridays influenced the consumption of crawfish. *Ashton Roberthon family*.

A cool front moved in during the early morning of April 10, and a steady rain cast a gloom over the weekend events. "When I saw that rain this morning, I could have cried," said Mayor Kern.[138]

At 9:00 a.m., Bishop Maurice Schexnayder began the Pontifical Mass at St. Bernard and read a papal greeting from Pope John XXIII bestowing apostolic blessing "upon the faithful, their families and all attending the centennial." With the blessing bestowed, the clouds parted and cooler-than-usual temperatures made the day suddenly perfect for the celebration.[139]

Not to be outdone by the church, French consul general Jacques Grellet presented a French flag to Mayor Kern and led everyone in the singing of the "La Marseillaise," the French national anthem. President Dwight Eisenhower also sent his congratulations to the town with a wire that read, "Located in the historic Acadian section of Louisiana, your city helped to preserve a great tradition for America."[140]

The Mass was followed by a blessing of the new city hall and the "Colored Parade," "colored" being the politically correct term of the time period for African Americans.[141] Other events included folk exhibits, a street dance called a *fais do-do* (fay doh-doh) by Cajuns, a cooking bee, a kangaroo court, a beard-judging contest, a beauty pageant and coronation ball for Miss Breaux Bridge, a political rally, a grand parade, the final beard- and costume-judging contest, the "Cutting of the Centennial Cake" and, finally, "Le Bal des Vieux [The Old Folk's Ball],"[142] where the oldest married couples of Breaux Bridge proudly promenaded in costume at the presentation.

Though muddy conditions forced the heavily anticipated political rally inside the Breaux Bridge High School Gymnasium, political fireworks ensued. The main attraction was the colorful Governor Long, and folks were wondering just how colorful the governor would be. The newspaper corps expected a peppery debate. "Those crawfish will be mighty hot and spicy, and there's no telling how hot the political oratory will get," Jim LaCaffinie of the *Morning Advocate* wrote in a preview article.

The biggest firecracker of the day was thrown by Jack Hayes, a Lafayette businessman. Governor Long, Hayes said, was making a "mockery of the Constitution." And he charged that the governor had no intention of seeking an unlawful reelection. "I think what Governor Long would really like to have is a weak governor absent most of the time," Hayes claimed. Hayes said Long would back musician Jimmie Davis, who would be too busy singing to do an effective job of governing the state. "With all of Davis' movies and records, Davis wouldn't have too much time to work in office…It would be a very sorry administration for the next four years," Hayes said.[143] He then parodied Long's speaking manner as he said Long's ultimate plan was to return in four years to save the state. "Ol' Earl is battle-scarred and weary; and I am 67 years old now, weary of war, but I'm going to sacrifice another four years to put you out of this mess you got yourselves into."[144]

Hayes spoke past his allotted twelve minutes, but the amused Long hollered out, "Give him some extra time." "Okay, thanks very much,

Governor Earl K. Long, sporting a crawfish lapel pin, brought a lot of attention to Breaux Bridge when he appeared at the political rally at the town's centennial celebration. *Ashton Roberthon family.*

governor," Hayes responded. Later, the two men joked amiably on the stage after the rally.[145]

Expected mudslinging between Long and local favorite son Wade O. Martin, the incumbent Louisiana secretary of state, failed to materialize because Martin declined to attend. The "Singing Governor," Jimmie Davis, declining to announce his candidacy, said the only reason he was in Breaux Bridge was for the crawfish. "Crawfish bisque is my favorite dish…I often come back to Breaux Bridge for crawfish," he said.[146]

Long, sporting a crawfish pin on his lapel and in "mid-campaign" form,[147] touched on teacher tenure, dope peddlers, gas and "sulphur people" and railed against the *Times-Picayune*. "If the *Picayune* could rule, there would be no child getting free lunches, and none of our children would get a free college education," Long said. He expressed his wish that New Orleans mayor deLesseps "Chep" Morrison would enter the race. "I'm hoping and praying that Delussups [*sic*] Morrison in New Orleans will run. With your help I want to give that little squirt another beating before I die."[148]

Not one to let Long's dig at the *Picayune* go unnoticed, editor Pete Baird compared Long to a shell stuffed for crawfish bisque: "The big question at the Breaux Bridge crawfish festival was what Ole Earl's head is stuffed with."[149]

Breaux Bridge Centennial Celebration chairman Raymond Castille and his wife, Maxine, attended all the social events that Long was invited to, including a crawfish bisque dinner at the Louisiana Agriculture Building on Court Street. They didn't know that Long, during that period of his life, had been "act[ing] like an eighteen-year-old boy who had just left the family farm and had discovered New Orleans for the first time."[150]

Years later, in a 2013 interview, they both grinned slyly when asked about the governor's behavior. Raymond would say only that "the governor cut up."[151] Cutting up is a gentleman's description of "We really tied one on last night." Maxine acknowledged that Long had a few drinks but that he generally kept them concealed as much as possible.[152]

By all accounts, Breaux Bridge's Centennial Celebration and, by extension, the celebration of the crawfish, was an overwhelming success. Boiled crawfish was served "almost continuously from a stand set up behind the Fire Station and also during the grand parade, boiled crawfish was thrown as 'favors' to grappling spectators along the way. Even the dignitaries in the reviewing stand, which included Gov. Earl K. Long, reached out for some."[153]

The *Teche News* reported that "thousands and thousands of persons poured into Breaux Bridge,"[154] but the *Morning Advocate* estimated the centennial draw at seventy-five thousand.[155] The *Picayune* pegged the crowd at only twenty thousand.[156] No matter the attendance, everyone applauded eighteen-year-old Diane Domingues (her Cajunized Spanish name is pronounced *doh-mangz*), who won the title of Miss Breaux Bridge.[157] Subsequent queens of the Crawfish Festival are named the Crawfish Queen, but Domingues is and will always be Miss Breaux Bridge, Centennial Queen.

Years later, on the thirtieth anniversary of the Crawfish Festival, centennial publicity chairman Ashton Roberthon would reflect that one of the positives about the town's birthday was that no one was arrested.[158] While that may

Orel Guidry, Doc Dautrieve and John Allen Breaux prepare the "world's greatest crawfish boil" at the Breaux Bridge Centennial. The water is heated with a wood fire. *Ashton Roberthon family.*

be an astonishing statistic given that the town was crammed with upwards of twenty thousand beer-drinking crawfish eaters, Blackie Bienvenu of the *Teche News* saw more significance in the event just a week after the show was over. "I have never seen so many people working together, without friction, all for a single purpose to tell the world of their wonderful town, area and

Breaux Bridge Centennial Queen Diane Domingues is toasted by Parade Chairman John Breaux at the town's 1959 Centennial Celebration. *LDAF.*

their wonderful way of life," Bienvenu said. "It is a tribute to a community to have staged such a giant celebration so wonderfully."[159]

But how did the "world" view the Centennial Celebration? The *Morning Advocate*'s Jim LaCaffinie may have said it best:

> *The centennial put Breaux Bridge on the map indisputably. National and state press and other media coverage carried the town's centennial across the nation this weekend as the community mixed a dash of politics at a gubernatorial rally with her "joie de vivre." For a good measure, the town threw in some boiled crawfish...*
>
> *These events revitalized the community's interest in its heritage and past history, brought the people closer together in an all-town affair...and won recognition for Breaux Bridge as a strong, enduring part of Louisiana. In turn, Louisiana was enhanced immeasurably from the nationwide spotlight which fell upon one of her communities.*[160]

Breaux Bridge and the tiny crawfish were a hit.

THE ORIGINAL ÉTOUFFÉE:
MRS. CHARLES HEBERT AND ALINE GUIDRY
CHAMPAGNE'S CRAWFISH ÉTOUFFÉE

1 cup onion, chopped
2 tablespoons oil
¾ cup water
1 cup crawfish tail meat with fat
1 rounded tablespoon flour
Paprika, salt and red and black pepper to taste
Parsley and green onion, chopped for garnish

Sauté onion in oil until golden and tender. Add water and tails with fat. Simmer for fifteen to twenty minutes. Thicken with flour and then add seasonings to taste. Serve over white rice. Garnish with parsley and green onion. (Used with permission from Terry Harris Champagne.)

CHAPTER 4

ETERNAL KING CRAWFISH

Crawfish made a successful debut during the 1959 Breaux Bridge Centennial Celebration due to the pride town residents had for their community. But the crawfish hole is deep, and many famous and not-so-famous colorful personalities also boosted the Cajun crustacean's popularity. Certainly, there are no shortages of colorful personalities in south Louisiana.

Governor Earl K. Long's visit to the city upped the recognition quotient of the crawfish. And Jimmie Davis, the crooner-turned-governor who politicked at the centennial, absolutely loved crawfish. He ate crawfish étouffée nearly every day at Westmoreland Piccadilly Cafeteria in Baton Rouge after retiring from politics.[161] These two outsized political personalities drew a lot of attention to crawfish, but they paled in comparison to the eccentricity and audacity of Leon Leo Breaux, a local restaurateur who brashly proclaimed himself "Eternal King Crawfish" in the months leading up to the 1960 festival.

Leon's father, Dudley "T-Nu" Breaux, had done well selling secondhand auto parts during World War II, and the family maintained Breaux's One-Stop on Berard Street for many years. One could eat a "plate lunch" for dinner (as Cajuns call the noon meal) while having the gas tank filled or a bicycle tire repaired. Leon or his presumed autistic brother, Lee, would come to the table and recite the lunch menu choices. The fare was typical for southwestern Louisiana: stewed seven steaks and smothered chicken with rice and gravy accompanied by white beans, butter beans or *haricots verts* (green beans).

T-Nu was hard on his three sons—Bucky, Leon and Lee—and often denigrated the boys in front of customers. He said that Lee was probably the "smartest one in the whole bunch," but he did love Leon enough to buy him a black Packard convertible in 1948.[162]

Leon was active in civic clubs. He served as the secretary-treasurer of the Lion's Club in 1957[163] and attended the Lion's International conventions in New York City in 1954 and Miami the following year. Wherever he traveled, "he told people about the good Cajun cooking in south Louisiana and crawfish."[164]

Perhaps he thought his spot in the town society was a rung too low because he was fond of referring to the powers that be in Pont Breaux as "the clique." He constantly mentioned various "mockeries of justice" that may or may not have happened to him. While many Cajuns referred to outsiders as "Americains," Leon called any new arrival to the town, French-speaking or not, an "immigrant."[165] His manner was sometimes boorish, and he was prone to scratch himself inappropriately in public or clear phlegm from his throat a bit too loudly for most folks' sensibilities.[166] But he was also a direct descendant of Firmin Breaux, patriarch of the founding family of Breaux Bridge, and played an active role in the town's society.

Despite his peccadilloes, Leon was an average guy who probably wouldn't have made any special mark on the world but for the siren call of the crawfish. He shamelessly seized upon the celebration of the crustacean as a vehicle for his self-invented celebrity. He started by proclaiming himself the Eternal King Crawfish. Not King Leon the Crawfish King, which might have implied there would be a King Clovis, King Aristile or King Mulate, but Eternal King Crawfish—*eternal* unequivocally implying *forever*. Sometime before St. Patrick's Day 1960, Leon let it be known to J.S. Badon (pronounced *bah-dawnh*), the Breaux Bridge correspondent to the *Teche News*, that he was the Eternal King Crawfish. He didn't leak the information—he placed it, and Badon bit.

Leon slyly linked his rising star to Anna Belle Dupuis Hoffman, *la grande dame* who helped launch Breaux Bridge's successful Centennial Celebration. Miss Anna Belle famously tooled around Breaux Bridge in "Antiquity," her Model A adorned with a crest painted by artists Al Manning and Woodrow Marshall, also of Centennial celebrity. If the old lady could have a crest, so could the emerging Eternal King Crawfish.

"Al Manning and Woody Marshall are at it again," Badon wrote in his weekly missive. "This time they are creating a crest for Leon Breaux, King Crawfish." King Crawfish? Most likely the one-paragraph news article elicited responses of incredulity in the town's barbershop chairs and under the beauty shop hair dryers. "Leon? *Mais, c'est fou* (but, that's nuts)" was probably the reaction of local folks, said Jack Dale Delhomme, a high school student at the time of Leon's self-appointment.[167]

By nature, high school students seek out the outrageous, the extreme and the risky, and in Leon, Jack Dale and his teenage crew found someone who seemed to be thumbing a nose at "the clique."

"We called him King—King Leon Breaux, the crawfish king—and it started catching on with my age group," Delhomme said. "And every time we'd see him, we'd say, 'Look, it's the king—the Crawfish King. Whatta you say?"[168]

And why couldn't Leon assume the mantle of crawfish king? He had that one thing—the same thing that makes the crawfish lift up its claws in the face of an onrushing locomotive: courage.

Louisiana is famous for kings. The Napoleon House was built for the emperor himself to live in.[169] But Napoleon never arrived, so the state did the next best thing—it created Mardi Gras and Rex, the king of Carnival. Louisiana loves kings. Louisiana has the Boudin King, the Boogie Kings, King Creole, the King of Zydeco, the Cast Net King, king cakes and king snakes. And in 1960, Breaux Bridge had its own king, the Eternal King Crawfish, Leon Leo Breaux, appointed by, well, himself—but a king nonetheless.

There was even a coronation of sorts.

The Veterans Home had been the setting for many a fundraising centennial dance, and Leon chose the venue for his coming-out party by enlisting the help of the elected royalty, Miss Breaux Bridge, Dianne Domingues, daughter of Mr. and Mrs. Ethel Champagne Domingues and R.D. "Papoot" Domingues.

"We lived next door to them [the Breaux family]," said Dianne. "I guess he wanted to be the first king, and he asked me. I think he came to the house."[170]

She brought along her court, the lovely Irene Delhomme (aunt of NFL quarterback Jake Delhomme) and beautiful Barbara Harrington, to participate in a photo session with Manning and Marshall behind the lens.

Reporter J.S. Badon, stringing for the *Picayune*, filed a story for Howard Jacobs's "Remoulade" column:

> *Leon Leo Breaux, young "King Crawfish of Breaux Bridge," finally got his wish.*
>
> *The picture taking lasted two hours, with Leon in a clean tuxedo and the girls crowning him with a jeweled crown and scepter. All kinds of poses of standing and sitting types beside the huge crawfish placard bearing Leon's*

name and crest. Guests and friends had gathered at the Vets' home to bend elbows and watch the picture taking.

All went well until the finale. Then it was decided to end the long sequence by having Leon crowned with a bucket of live crawfish.

Domingues poured the live bucket of crawling crawfish over him and his freshly cleaned tuxedo to the laughter and cheers of the gang. The end. Al and Woodrow used floodlights, and the effect was dazzling. Mr. Breaux is now ETERNAL KING CRAWFISH. He says he will reign forever.[171]

By this act, Leon was symbolically taking on the form of the crawfish. There are many cases of people assuming animal form in mythology and folklore. Zeus was forever transforming his mistresses into cows so that he could avoid the wrath of his wife. The Cajun mother called on the *rougarou*, a lycanthropic creature with the body of a man and head of a wolf, to frighten her children into good behavior. If Leon Breaux wanted to assume the role of crawfish king, so what? He certainly made a wise choice.

More so than shrimp, crabs, oysters or alligators, Leon innately knew that the crawfish was greater than something that was just good to eat. Leon recognized, as Cajun radio broadcaster Revon Reed wrote later in *Lâche Pas la Patate*, that "the crawfish symbolized many things for the Cajun: money in the bank, the food in his belly, bravery, and power for the politician. The crawfish affects the whole Cajun culture."[172] In short, Leon believed that the crawfish was everything that was right about the Cajun culture.

During his reign, Leon tirelessly promoted the crawfish, the Crawfish Festival, Breaux Bridge, Cajunism, Louisiana and himself. He started by inserting himself at the head of every Crawfish Festival parade beginning in 1960 until his death in 1981. Leon, possibly thumbing his nose at the "clique," performed his kingly duties outside the auspices of the Crawfish Festival Association organizers.

"They didn't necessarily want Leon to lead the parade, so he would park his car on a side street," said Harris "Buddy" Pellerin, a regular diner at Breaux's One-Stop. "When the color guard would pass, Leon's driver would ease into the flow and head the parade."[173]

Wearing his crown, cape and brandishing his scepter about, Leon entered Le Roux, his magnificent racing crawfish, in the inaugural Crawfish Derby during the 1960 festival. He helped hype the race by sending an item to Blackie Bienvenu of the *Teche News* comparing his crawfish to LSU's Heisman Trophy winner Billy Cannon. "Leon Breaux, self-styled 'Eternal King Crawfish' of Breaux Bridge, has been training his crawfish Le Roux for the

The coronation of Eternal King Crawfish Leon Leo Breaux by Miss Breaux Bridge Centennial Queen Dianne Domingues in 1960. *Dianne Domingues*.

The crawfish races at the 1969 Breaux Bridge Crafwish Festival. The winners escaped the boiling pot but ended up immortalized on plaques. *State Library of Louisiana.*

crawfish races to be held after High Mass next to the Farmers & Merchants Bank on Sunday. Leon says Le Roux is not as fast as Billy Cannon but he can sure travel all kinds of ways," wrote Blackie.[174]

Getting a mention in the weekly *Teche News* of St. Martin Parish was a beginning, but Leon set his sights on something grander, something more befitting of crawfish royalty. He commissioned artist Manning to paint an "ultra-modernistic" mural in his restaurant of a new planet envisioned by the Eternal King Crawfish. The 1961 mural depicted an exploding earth destroyed by nuclear bomb and the "King's plan to escape from such a calamity to a new planet of his own design." Again, Leon enlisted the aid of the Centennial Queen and newly crowned 1960 Crawfish Queen Emmaline Hebert to pose in a publicity photograph published by at least one state newspaper.[175]

In Leon's mind, it was "anything to get publicity." To others, it just confirmed that Leon was *plein fou* (very nutty).

Gene Mearns, a young Louisiana newspaperman when Leon arrived on the scene, appreciated the king's appeal. "I was working for UPI then and covering the state capitol beat," Mearns said in a 2013 interview. "Leon Leo

Breaux, the Eternal Crawfish King, came out to address the Senate. He wore the tuxedo, the crown and the cape. He had a radar—he could single out the press. He had a desire to know who you were. He was guileless, an open soul. I think he was a bit mad."[176]

Teche News publisher Ken Grissom said he was astonished when Leon showed up at Lafayette's *Daily Advertiser* office years ago dressed in full royal regalia. "I cannot conceive of anybody of that age and ilk walking around in a crown let alone all the other stuff that they put on except during Mardi Gras," Grissom said. "That always seemed weird to me, but here's Leon, it's not even Mardi Gras, and he's wearing a crown."[177]

Leon's greatest public relations feat, however, was the concept of rewarding his loyal subjects, near and far, with a commemoration of their achievements. At the 1960 St. Bernard Athletics Association Boat Races, Leon bestowed upon Emmaline Hebert, the newly anointed Breaux Bridge Crawfish Queen, a plaque mounted with a crawfish. The presentation was mentioned in statewide newspapers.[178]

Realizing he could get media attention with the plaque gimmick and thus bring publicity to the nascent Crawfish Festival, Leon began to hand out the awards left and right. His road show took him to the 1962 Sugar Cane Festival in New Iberia, where he gave the outgoing Sugar Queen a plaque.[179] He traveled to Shreveport, a five-hour trip from Breaux Bridge, to give the national president of the Jaycees civic organization a plaque.[180] In Abbeville, he awarded the retiring 1963 Dairy Queen with the souvenir.

Morning Advocate reporter Jim LaCaffanie, who had covered the 1959 Centennial Celebration, was well aware of the Eternal Crawfish King. In his Dairy Festival coverage, LaCaffanie wrote, "Among the visiting royalty were Breaux Bridge's Crawfish King, Leon Leo Breaux, who presented awards to the retiring queen and to one of the judges, Johnny Beazley, Louisiana native and former major-league pitcher."

Dressed in royal raiment, he presented Houston Astros owner Judge Roy Hoffeinz with a crawfish plaque on home plate in the Astrodome on Cajun Day in 1964.

There's no official count of how many plaques the Eternal King Crawfish doled out, but Brenda Broussard, the 1967 Crawfish Queen, said Leon may have pulled a fast one with her. "I remember posing for a photograph with him presenting me with the plaque, but Leon never actually gave it to me," Broussard said.[181]

The Eternal King Crawfish began crashing or receiving invites to area Mardi Gras balls, festivals, beauty pageants and meetings[182] and was honored by politicians. Nearly all welcomed him with at least an introduction and a walk-through. In 1972, Governor Edwin Edwards, perhaps the most popular governor in Louisiana history, awarded Leon the first honorary Colonel's Commission of his administration.[183] The king was pictured in state papers claiming the first-issued automobile license plate for State Police Troop I in 1965[184] and Troop C three years later.[185]

Photographed with kings, queens and politicians,[186] the colorful Leon was always good for a crawfish quote. In a UPI article, Leon mentions the abdication of the 1966 queen, who chose to get married. "Queens may come and queens may go, but Eternal King Crawfish shall reign forever," Leon said.[187]

Royal decrees were also issued, and Associate Justice Frank W. Summers of the Louisiana Supreme Court was enlisted to witness Leon's 1968 "World Proclamation of Crawfish for Eternity." The *Morning Advocate* reported, "The Eternal King Crawfish Leon Leo Breaux proclaimed the opening of the 1966 Crawfish Season, not a Crawfish Day or a Crawfish Week or a Crawfish Month in the Crawfish Capital of Louisiana, but he went and proclaimed his proclamations much further, as to state and proclaim Crawfish Year International for Eternity."[188]

Obviously, there was a whole lot of proclaiming going on when Leon was Eternal King Crawfish.

Leon's legacy is not forgotten by the residents of Breaux Bridge. The *Teche News* featured articles on Leon in Crawfish Festival supplements in 1978 and again after his death. "Leon Leo Breaux of Breaux Bridge has probably traveled more miles and made more appearances on behalf of the Crawfish Festival than any other person. He presented literally hundreds of crawfish plaques to dignitaries from near and far," said the St. Martinville newspaper.[189]

Breaux Bridge mayor Jack Dale Delhomme, still grateful for the cash Leon paid him for being his parade driver fifty years ago, believes the Eternal King Crawfish should be eternally remembered. "Leon was a good ambassador to the City of Breaux Bridge," Delhomme said. "The crawfish gave us notoriety—we are the Crawfish Capital. Next to New Orleans, I believe Breaux Bridge is the most identifiable town in Louisiana. Some people frowned upon Leon because he was different. It wasn't until I became associated with Leon [and started] driving him in parades that I realized where this guy was coming from. Leon was the king. Leon had nerve. He wasn't afraid to say, 'I'm Leon Breaux, and I'm Crawfish King—the Eternal Crawfish King. Come visit Breaux Bridge.'"[190]

It's fitting that no one assumed the kingship after Leon's death in 1981. It takes nerve, time and money to be the Crawfish King, and Leon paid for all of his town-promoting activities out of his own pocket.[191]

Leon's famous crown, cape and scepter were displayed at his funeral wake, but he was not buried in his regal attire, as some believe.[192] For some time, the royal accoutrements were on display at Café des Amis, which is owned and operated by Leon's cousin Dickie Breaux, but the current whereabouts of the items are unknown.[193] The mural of the Eternal King Crawfish's imaginary planet was destroyed when Breaux's One-Stop was demolished in the 1980s.

Realizing the potential a Crawfish King had for the Crawfish Festival and the town, the Crawfish Festival Association reclaimed the title in 1989 when it appointed former Breaux Bridge mayor Louis Kern King Crawfish. Incidentally, Robert "Bob" K. Irwin, the author's father, reigned over the 1993 festival as King Crawfish. Others have honorably fulfilled their one-year appointments as King Crawfish, but there will be only one Eternal King Crawfish, and Leon Leo Breaux's name will be revered in the crawfish pantheon for, well, eternity.

Even King Louis XIII was sometimes bested by Cardinal Richelieu. Shared here is the famous haute cuisine Crawfish Cardinale recipe of Antoine's Restaurant in New Orleans, as published in *The New Orleans Cookbook*. The recipe is used with the permission of Chef Michael Regua of Antoine's.

CRAWFISH CARDINALE

5 tablespoons salt butter
⅓ cup finely chopped onion
2 tablespoons flour
¼ cup heavy cream
¾ cup milk
1 cup crawfish tails (about 20 tails)
¾ teaspoon salt
¼ teaspoon freshly ground white pepper
¼ teaspoon cayenne

$^1/_8$ teaspoon mace

$^1/_8$ teaspoon allspice

$^1/_8$ teaspoon cloves

1 whole bay leaf, crushed

3 tablespoons cognac

1 tablespoon dry white wine

1 tablespoon finely minced fresh parsley

$^1/_4$ teaspoon finely minced garlic

In a small heavy skillet or sauté pan, melt two tablespoons of the butter over low heat. Add the onion and sauté until soft and glazed but not brown. In large heavy skillet or sauté pan, melt the remaining three tablespoons of butter, add the flour and cook over low heat, stirring constantly until a light yellow roux is formed. Turn off the heat, add the contents of the small skillet to the roux and slowly blend in the cream and milk. Turn the heat to very low and cook until the mixture thickens, stirring constantly. Add the crawfish tails and mix well. Stir in the salt, pepper, cayenne, mace, allspice, cloves and bay leaf. Add the cognac and white wine and simmer over very low heat, stirring constantly for about four minutes. Sprinkle in the minced parsley and garlic and simmer for ten to twelve minutes to allow the seasonings to expand. The mixture should be stirred frequently with a wooden spoon to prevent scorching or sticking. Serve in heated individual ramekins or gratin dishes.[194]

CHAPTER 5

WHY DID THE CRAWFISH CROSS THE ROAD?

In 1933, the *New York Times* printed a story titled "Crawfish Blacken Road." The Associated Press piece reported on a huge "crawfish run," which it termed a "zoological phenomenon which occurs at rare intervals in Louisiana." The August 7 incident occurred on U.S. 61 between Gramercy and New Orleans. The unknown AP author wrote, "Superintendent E.P. Roy of the State Highway Patrol said the road was black for five miles with crawfish migrating from a swamp on one side of the road to low country on the other side, apparently motivated by a desire for more food."[195] Louisiana motorists of all stripes—Cajun, Creole and *Américain*—knew exactly what to do. "Many persons were filling sacks, assuring pots of succulent bisque and gumbo, while thousands of the crawfish were being crushed by highway traffic."[196]

The *New York Times* picking up a story from a *Baton Rouge State-Times* report was not exactly unusual. New York had a bit of a crawfish market. Besides, irrepressible Governor Huey Long, who often wore his pajamas to receive distinguished guests, had put Louisiana on the map.[197] National editors kept a collective eye on the newswire from Baton Rouge and were happy to include a quirky story about crawfish in the newspaper.

In 1952, a United Press story with the curious headline "Gourmet's Day on Highways" ran in the *Oxnard Press-Courier*. The California newspaper reported that "roads west of New Orleans were literally covered today with a layer of the principal ingredient of a Louisiana delicacy, crayfish bisque."

Again, savvy Louisiana residents harvested the jubilee. "Crayfish by the tens of thousands began crossing U.S. Highway [*sic*] around

CRAWFISH BLACKEN ROAD.

Rare 'Run' Covers Miles of Louisiana Highway.

BATON ROUGE, La., Aug. 7 (Æ). —A huge "crawfish run," zoological phenomenon which occurs at rare intervals in Louisiana, today was reported under way on the New Orleans-Baton Rouge highway near Gramercy. Millions of crawfish engage in such runs. Many persons were filling sacks, assuring pots of succulent bisque and gumbo, while thousands of the crawfish were being crushed by highway traffic.

Superintendent E. P. Roy of the State Highway Patrol said the road was black for five miles with crawfish migrating from a swamp on one side of the road to low country on the other side, apparently motivated by a desire for more food.

News of a 1933 crawfish migration made the *New York Times* and other newspapers in this Associated Press clipping. Locals, of course, scooped up the wayward crawfish and cooked gumbo. *Associated Press.*

noon yesterday. Motorists had to stop. When they saw what was covering the highway, containers of all kinds were brought out to take the meaty crustaceans home," said the *Courier*.[198]

Louisiana biologist Percy Viosca Jr., an early crawfish researcher, surmised, "The crayfish crossed the road because high tides or heavy rains in the low country have raised the water level of the holes where crawfish breed."[199]

James A. Daigle of Eunice, St. Landry Parish, and his family had the good luck to come across a crawfish migration in rural Calcasieu (pronounced *kal-ka-shew*) Parish, south of Lake Charles. As young James recalled:

Many years past, probably 1958 or 1959, my parents decided to pay a visit to my father's sister and her family in a small community by the name of Chalkley, which is south of Lake Charles. My mother decided she needed a new dress for attending Sunday Mass at the local country church.

We spent an uneventful weekend and headed for home after nightfall on Sunday. In those days, the roads consisted of gravel surfaces in the countryside. Upon leaving their homeplace, we entered Pine Pasture Road and quickly noticed an odd scene. The gravel road was covered with migrating crawfish.

At this point, my father instructed my mother to take over the wheel and ordered me to retrieve a rice sack out of the trunk, as he always kept a sack and string for storing fish. He then instructed me to assist him with filling the sack with the largest black crawfish I had ever witnessed.

Upon completely filling the sack, he decided there were simply too many crawfish to quit the harvesting. He immediately walked back to the car and retrieved my mother's new dress from the backseat and tied the neck and sleeves securely, and we began filling this beautiful dress with crawfish.

At this point, my mother was not amused, and choice words were uttered most of the way home by my mother. It really was a long trip home, with utter silence from my sister and me.

My mother did buy a replacement dress the following week.[200]

Seafood market dealers in Breaux Bridge, Henderson, Catahoula, Pierre Part and Arnaudville were slowly developing a market for peeled crawfish tail meat and began to recognize a larger crawfish potential. Most of the crawfish consumed from the 1940s through the early '60s were harvested from the waters of the Atchafalaya Basin. The protection levees created higher flood levels and made it difficult for people to live along the Atchafalaya River. The increased water flow made the swampy area a veritable paradise for the crawfish to live and make baby crawfish. But there was a serpent in crawfish Eden—the swamp crop was unreliable. There would be boatloads of crawfish one year and just a bucketful the next.

In 1958, the basin crop was 668,300[201] pounds, the largest in ten years. Commercial fishermen who had heretofore made their living primarily with catfish, gaspergou and buffalo looked forward to the extra income crawfish provided. The year 1959 was going to be a good one—Breaux Bridge invited the world to help celebrate its 100th birthday, the market for peeled crawfish tail meat was expanding and the demand was rising. Fishermen invested in new traps and boats, but their hopes for a bonanza were dashed when the catch dipped to 285,000 pounds.[202] The year 1960 was a little better—the harvest was almost 500,000 pounds.

In crawfish world, everyone is an expert, and folks from New Orleans to New Iberia could offer an opinion not only about Tulane's chances against LSU in the annual grudge football game but also the price of tea in China, who was going to win the gubernatorial election and the reasons for the drop in crawfish production.

Al Scramuzza, the indefatigable New Orleans seafood merchant who created a larger market for the Cajun crustacean in the Crescent City, sometimes talked through his hat when speculating about crawfish. Scramuzza was Howard Jacobs's go-to man when it came to crawfish, and the "Nabob of Crawdadia"[203] was always happy to provide a quote, even if he didn't know the proper function of the Morganza Spillway. "We quoted crawdad tycoon Al Scramuzza Wednesday as saying there was a current shortage of the meaty little tidbits. He attributed it to the fact that high water spilling over the Morganza Spillway had dispersed the mudbugs," Jacobs wrote in a March 1961 "Remoulade" column.

The problem? In 1961, the Morganza Spillway was high and dry.

U.S. Army Corps of Engineers liaison Bruce Sassaman set the record straight when he reported to Jacobs that "no water has ever flowed over the Morganza Spillway. In fact, it has never been opened. Actually, the water is two feet below the levee in front of the Morganza control structure."[204]

In all likelihood, Scramuzza misspoke about the Morganza Spillway. The Morganza Spillway floodgates, when opened, funnel water down into the Atchafalaya Spillway, which was the term most folks used to describe the Atchafalaya Basin in the 1960s. (Incidentally, the Morganza Spillway has been wet only twice in its fifty-nine-year history—once in 1973, when wild crawfish production at 4.5 million pounds nearly doubled 1972's production,[205] and in the Great Mississippi River Flood of 2011, when wild production hit 9.5 million.)[206]

The value of the crawfish market was growing and estimated to have been worth more than $1 million in 1958.[207] By the time the 1960 Crawfish

Festival came around, folks in bayou country were plenty accustomed to speculating on the crawfish season.

Certainly, a lot of talk around the weight scales at Amy's Fisheries in Henderson, the bar at the Pierre Part's Rainbow Inn and the kitchen at Don's Seafood and Steakhouse in Lafayette must have centered on the crawfish.

"We don't know why the crawfish are not coming out this year," *Teche News* writer Blackie Bienvenu wrote in his March 19, 1959 "This and That" column. "Antoine Bourque of Catahoula told me yesterday that he and his buddy ran over 100 nets and picked up only 31 pounds of crawfish, not enough to pay even the boat expenses, much less the truck, traps and bait. This has been one of the worst seasons in history, and things don't look too good for the near future."[208]

Consider the numbers: the seventy-five thousand guests at the Breaux Bridge Centennial Celebration could have consumed the entire 1959 catch of 200,000 pounds in one weekend.

Contemplating a world without crawfish, members of the St. Martin Parish Sportsmen's Club did the only responsible thing: they called in a professional.

Viosca, who had now attained the lofty position of state biologist with the Louisiana Wildlife and Fisheries Commission, arrived in St. Martinville on the morning of May 15, 1959. The hopes and dreams of crawfishermen from Arnaudville to Belle River, seafood merchants from Henderson to Pierre Part and crawfish connoisseurs from Baton Rouge to Breaux Bridge rested on this man with the straw hat.

As a kid growing up in New Orleans, Viosca knew the value of hard work. He and his brother René sewed their own nets and caught crabs, shrimp and crawfish in what is now called New Orleans East. The Viosca boys rode their bicycles to the French Market (a thirty-mile round trip) to sell their catch. The fishing work helped pay for Viosca's college education, and he graduated from Tulane University in 1913 with a bachelor's degree in science. He earned a master's degree two years later. Viosca set up the Southern Biological Supply Company, which provided crawfish to dissection laboratory students across the country.[209]

Viosca first appeared on the public crawfish scene in 1922, when he claimed second place in an "open championship tournament" of crawfish eating in the French Market. He claimed that he should have won the contest because the "Vieux Carré champion" had not "licked the shells clean."[210] Obviously, multicultural Crescent City residents of the Roaring Twenties, just like the Cajuns and Creoles of Pierre Part and Catahoula, loved their crawfish.

On February 4, 1933, the *Times-Picayune* observed the following:

Crawfish are to be had at any restaurant in town, prepared in a variety of ways. Half of the crawfish eaten in New Orleans, however, are not bought, but caught by the children of a family for amusement. A small child can easily catch sufficient for a family, if living in the vicinity of a crawfish section. Usually the food is simply boiled and cayenne peppered, and this method of preparation was preferred by many gourmets, at least when claré wine was easily obtained. Many old residents declare that crawfish lose much of their flavor unless accompanied by a bottle of vin rouge. *These say prohibition has destroyed much of the attractiveness and delight of timbale of crawfish.*[211]

But developers were expanding New Orleans, draining swamp and eliminating crawfish holes. In 1923, New Orleans residents fearful of eating their crawfish supply out of existence turned to the Department of Conservation. In a long *Times-Picayune* article complete with a banner headline and six photographs, agency director Carleton F. Pool assured them that even though there was "no more crawfishing now in city proper," the crawfish future was bright. He cited Viosca's "exhaustive study of the species, and found that the crawfish needed no protection whatever, being amply able to care for himself."[212]

Pool and Viosca predicted that there "will be no need for 'farms,' however, until all swamps, ponds and ditches of Louisiana become dried up through drainage." The residents along Hagan Avenue, one block off Orleans Avenue, knew about drainage.[213]

"Drainage has driven the crawfish farther and farther from the center of the city," Pool wrote, "and as years pass, the crawfishing parties have to go farther afield for them. There are any number of persons…who went in search of the 'mud bugs' afoot and found them in abundance in Hagan Avenue and at even nearer points. Now the trip is usually made to Shrewsbury, Kenner or to St. Bernard and Gentilly in automobiles."[214]

But Poole was optimistic that crawfish could be farmed in the future:

An acre of flat land in the neighborhood of a stream—and there are millions of such acres along the Mississippi—will, it has been calculated, produce 10,000 pounds of crawfish in a season. The average price of crawfish is ten cents a pound, the range during the season, according to supply, being from five to fifteen cents a pound. This figures out a possible *production of $1,000 an acre under intensive cultivation, but this profit could not be maintained on the present basis of values because such profits would induce so much competition that the production would soon outstrip the demand and price would topple as a consequence.* [215]

Viosca's crawfish credentials were unquestioned, but he was also very entrepreneurial, media savvy and a bit of a showman. He entered bullfrogs in a Mark Twain frog-jumping contest in New York[216] and enticed *Picayune* writer Evelyn E. Jones to write a fashion bit about the costume jewelry made from dried garfish scales, which he called "gar-ivory."[217] He was always good for a quote.

Viosca wrote about the virtues of crawfish as he studied the practices of Louisiana swampers and farmers. Crawfish ate the roots of the water hyacinths and could help control the invasive plant.[218] They fed on mosquito larvae, keeping the population of the malaria-causing insect down.[219] He wrote about the "super crayfish from Pierre Part"[220] for *Dixie* magazine and monitored the crawfish aqua-cultivation efforts of Acadia Parish rice farmer Voorhies Trahan (pronounced *Traw-haan*), who, in 1948, was the first to commercially rotate a rice crop with crawfish.[221]

So what had happened to the 1959 crawfish catch? On the morning of May 15, Viosca met Leo Dautrieve of the Sportsmen's Club and game wardens Robert Romero, Leo Bulliard Jr. and Melvin Dupuis in St. Martinville. For two days, he toured the Atchafalaya Spillway and visited Lake Fausse Point. The trip took him into Grand Lake and then back to Mud Cove. At noon, the group stopped at Buffalo Cove, where they were met by other Sportsman's Club members. After a fish dinner, the group inspected the Benoit area, Bayou Chene, Tensas, Butte la Rose and other spots "where commercial fishermen seek crawfish." That night, a general meeting with commercial fishermen, seafood buyers and restaurateurs was held at Robin's Seafood House in Henderson.[222]

Viosca's initial thoughts on improving future catches included a six-month closed season during the crawfish spawning season and the use of a larger trap that would allow smaller crawfish to escape. He recommended that Wildlife and Fisheries appoint a full-time biologist to study the situation, while Dean Joe Riehl of Southwestern Louisiana Institute (now the University of Louisiana at Lafayette) said the school's biology department had "already started investigating the life cycle of the crawfish and seeking the solution for the shortage."[223]

Viosca thought "many things could account for the lack of crawfish this year." The fishermen and buyers had their thoughts, too, among which "included the taking of crawfish too late last year, stagnant water, sand bars, shocking machines, and poison for fire ants control."[224] Viosca discounted those ideas. He already knew the answer—he just had to check some other numbers before making a final statement.

Before he left Robin's with a bellyful of Cajun cooking, Viosca gave the fishermen a clue: "Rainfall all over the Mississippi Valley could help determine the crawfish crop. Too much or too little water at the right time can hurt the crawfish," he said.[225]

The following year, Representative Robert "Bob" Angelle got the Louisiana legislature to appropriate $10,000 to build Viosca a crawfish farm in Cecilia.

Crawfish Jambalaya is an underrated Cajun dish. Following is the recipe that was featured in the Breaux Bridge Crawfish Festival program.

CRAWFISH JAMBALAYA

3 pounds crawfish tails
2 blocks butter
2 tablespoons flour
6 onions, shredded
Chopped parsley
Chopped onion tops
3 cups cooked rice
Salt, black pepper and red pepper to season

Melt butter and add flour. Brown a little bit. Add onions and cook until soft. Add fat from crawfish. (To get fat today, make sure you buy fresh, never-frozen, Louisiana crawfish. Remove the crawfish from bag and set aside. Add a tablespoon of water to the bag to salvage the fat from the bag.) Let simmer for a few more minutes and then add tails, parsley, onion tops and seasonings. Cook fifteen minutes. When ready to serve, add cooked rice and mix.

CHAPTER 6

FESTIVAL TURMOIL

Not satisfied with introducing crawfish to the world in the 1959 centennial and the subsequent 1960 Crawfish Festival, Breaux Bridge decided to secede from the Union. In 1962, Breaux Bridge issued *A Declaration by the Citizens of Breaux Bridge, Louisiana in Congress Assembled*,[226] which marked its intent to secede from the United States—at least for the weekend. Some might chalk up this drastic move to the temporary insanity often caused by the prospect of crawfish consumption, but the more likely reason was the festival's "Spirit of the Confederacy" theme.[227]

The story "Breaux Bridge Cajuns Revolt Against Non-Crawfish World" in the *Port Arthur News* was significant because the press release embraced Cajun French Louisiana's distinct qualities. Those distinctions were often ridiculed by English speakers,[228] but Breaux Bridge was nurturing a nascent pride of Cajunism.[229]

The declaration, naturally, was tongue in cheek and used terminology that only a Cajun would completely understand:

A Declaration by the Citizens of Breaux Bridge,
Louisiana in Congress Assembled

When, in the course of human events, it becomes necessary for one people, namely, we Cajuns of Breaux Bridge, to cast off the oppressive yoke of a comparatively joyless and doleful state and nation, then therefore and to wit does it behoove us to set forth the reasons for our actions.

We find that the majority of the citizens of this state and nation are incompatible with us in that:

1. *They do not eat couche-couche.*
2. *They cannot make, much less do they eat, gratons and boudin.*
3. *They cannot make a decent crawfish stew or étouffée.*
4. *They cannot cook grillades a la chique.*
5. *They cannot cook nor do they eat court bouillon de poisson.*
6. *They murder what should be good gumbo.*
7. *They are not disciples of Epicurus.*
8. *They cannot dance a fais do-do.*
9. *They cannot let Le Bon Temps Rouler.*
10. *They cannot speak Cajun.*

For the forgoing reasons, we the people of Breaux Bridge, giving vent to a rebellious exuberance and a joie de vivre which set us apart from state and nation, do hereby declare our intent to secede from the state of Louisiana and the United States of America and establish our independence as a hilariously free nation: the Kingdom of Breaux Bridge, Crawfish Capital of the World—La Capitale Mondiale des Écrevisse.

This act of secession is effective on April 27, 28, 29, 1962, after which time we shall revert to exhaustedly satisfied and docile citizens of our state and nation.

It is our intention to seal off our borders during this three-day period with a Crawfish-Net Curtain and defend them against all invasions, permitting entry only to sympathetic people and honorary citizens with suitable passports.

In witness thereof, we, the undersigned patriots, do pledge our fortunes and our best stock of invigorating spirits and proclaim, "Laissez Le Bon Temps Rouler."[230]

Breaux Bridge residents knew their Cajun ethnicity was valuable and unique, and they were willing to share it with the world. Plus, Breaux Bridge had cornered the market on the crawfish as a symbol, and the crawfish proved to be an irresistible attractant—perhaps too good of an attractant.

The Bible says, "Man does not live by bread alone." The Breaux Bridge corollary to that verse was quoted by André Thevenet (pronounced *tev-nay*), one of the leading citizens of Breaux Bridge, who said, "A man who has not eaten crawfish has not lived."[231]

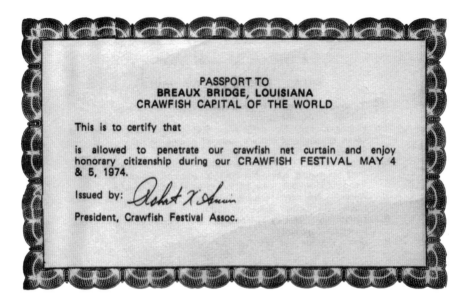

Wallet-size "passports" were given to visitors to the Breaux Bridge Crawfish Festival and allowed them to penetrate the "crawfish net curtain." *Grace Amy Irwin.*

And hundreds of thousands of people did want to eat crawfish and experience life to the fullest.

To penetrate the "Crawfish-Net Curtain," a play on the Cold War's "Iron Curtain," one had to possess a passport. "The passport, what a great marketing tool," said Ray Pellerin, the CFA president in 1966. "We had calls about that nearly every day."[232]

Woodrow Marshall, the commercial artist who had designed the town flag and other souvenirs for the centennial, came up with the unique concept of the crawfish races. The crawfish could be jockeyed by anyone who ponied up the entry fee. The clawed contestants were placed in the center of a target pattern of concentric circles painted on a plywood sheet. The first to reach the outer circle was the winner.

"It took me three years to perfect the crawfish races," Marshall said in 1968. "Knowing their habits, how they go forward and backward, I figure they want a bull's eye that they can go in any direction and get out of the circle. That is a genius stroke I had."[233]

Lafayette's KLFY-TV televised the inaugural 1960 races and paid particular attention to a special grudge crawfish race between Mayor Louis Kern and Don Landry of Don's Crawfish Ranch. Ashby Landry Sr. of Don's Seafood and Steakhouse in Lafayette had built a pond in

Ashby Landry of Don's Seafood and Steakhouse stands in front of Don's Crawfish Ranch. The actual "ranch" was 630 acres of wooded lowlands south of Henderson. *Don's Seafood and Steakhouse.*

1960 to supply the Landry restaurants with crawfish. Their crawfish ranch, "an industry peculiar to Louisiana," had generated significant publicity,[234] and the race coverage went out on a national radio feed.[235]

Kern actually went to the trouble of having a tiny jockey sculpted out of "play-clay" and affixed it to his crawfish's back. We've all heard of Thoroughbred racehorses breaking down on the turf, but this match was probably the first and only time a crawfish broke down at Crawfish Downs. "Mayor Kern's…huge crawfish, which was suspected of being a small lobster, died of a heart attack before the race ended. [The] crawfish collapsed under the weight of the saddle and jockey," reported the *Teche News.*[236]

A boat parade added in 1962 brought the celebration to the bayou. Local educator P.H. LeBlanc, along with his industrial arts class and Don Prejean (*pray-shawhn*) built a ten-foot crawfish to scale and mounted it atop a bateau. The crawfish, christened *Monsieur L'Écrevisse*, was an immediate hit and became the boat that launched a thousand photographs.

Police Chief Sidney "Line" Castille asked Carl Simon (*see-mawhn*) to "take over the Crawfish Festival" for 1964.[237] Simon, a young pharmacist whose family had owned a downtown retail store on Main Street for years, assumed the presidency of the CFA. With the festival already gaining popularity, Simon recruited other young professionals of Breaux Bridge and relied on the veterans from the 1959 and 1960 festivals. Together, they began to

The cover of the 1964 Breaux Bridge Crawfish Festival program features a drawing of an Acadian cottage. The 1964 festival president was Carl Simon, a downtown merchant. *Breaux Bridge Crawfish Festival Association.*

transform the festival from a celebration honoring the crawfish into a huge street party.

"I was associated with the Crawfish Festival Association for ten years," Simon said. "We were all young and socially connected. It would have been a Mardi Gras krewe if you had to relate it to something, but we never did make it a krewe. We had a dance, a contest, a parade and the ball."[238]

Breaux Bridge residents arriving by mule wagon at the 1959 centennial celebration's *fais do-do*. A *fais do-do* (Cajun French for "go to sleep") allowed children to play until they tired and napped while their parents danced. *Ashton Roberthon family.*

The group set up an administrative structure to keep the festival running. A president would serve a two-year term, after which he was succeeded by his vice-president.

"We kept perpetuating the festival," Simon said. "It became a Mardi Gras atmosphere—it was a party; the crawfish was just an excuse."[239]

The townspeople continued the tradition of dressing in nineteenth-century clothing, and the men grew their beards. Many of them participated in the newly created horse-and-buggy parade, which lent a quaint, old-timey air to the festivities.

Horses, however, bring their own set of problems, and by 1964, it had been decreed that none would be included in the Sunday parade. An exception was made for Governor Jimmie Davis's famous horse, a palomino named Sunshine in honor of Davis's hit song "You Are My Sunshine." The inclusion of Sunshine nearly wrecked the start of the 1964 Sunday parade and created a crack in the veneer of Crawfish Festival harmony.

"My parade chairman, Orel Ketelers, did not want Sunshine to be at the head of the parade," Simon said. "It was going to have BMs and the bands would have to walk through it."[240]

The matter was settled, Simon said, when Chief Castille, "being the politician that he was, he was *brute*, said the governor's horse will ride in the parade and I'm going to walk the horse."[241]

That was too much for Ketelers, who walked off the job.[242] Even though Ketelers was not impressed with Sunshine, *Morning Advocate* writer Ed Perez and the rest of the town were. "Among the leaders of the parade were Breaux Bridge's Mayor Louis Kern, astride a beautiful Palomino stallion, and the "Eternal Crawfish King," Leon Breaux, lifetime holder of the title," wrote Perez.[243]

The "outsiders" cited in Breaux Bridge's secession document who could not dance a *fais do-do* quickly learned. College fraternities from LSU and the University of Louisiana at Lafayette (then called University of Southwestern Louisiana) descended upon downtown Breaux Bridge with fervor.

Henry Barousse of Baton Rouge said many LSU Cajun students had suppressed their Acadian heritage to avoid appearing rural or unsophisticated, but the discovery of the Crawfish Festival set them free. "Along about 1963 or 1964, some fraternity boys from LSU discovered the Crawfish Festival in Breaux Bridge, and eating crawfish suddenly became trendy among the campus crowd," Barousse said.[244]

Crawfish also became trendy with Hollywood celebrities and jetsetters.

Ladies Home Journal journalist and etiquette mistress Amy Vanderbilt served as the Crawfish Queen pageant judge.[245] NFL football pros Jimmy Taylor of LSU and the Green Bay Packers and "Tall" Paul Guidry of the Buffalo Bills were contest judges.[246] Comedian Bill Dana brought his Jose Jimenez persona to the Crawfish Capital. Television news correspondent Dan Rather noted, "Crawfish Festival to the folks down here in Cajun country is what the Indianapolis 500 is to Indianapolis and what the Kentucky Derby is to the folks in bluegrass country."[247]

By 1966, the town had become so associated with crawfish that the local phone company featured a picture of a bright red crawfish on its directory. Up until 1974, a crawfish graced the directory cover every year save 1970.[248]

From the beginning, festival organizers highlighted tradition with Cajun French bands, cooking contests and Breaux Bridge's own special brand of joie de vivre. In addition to the crawfish races, merchant Robert Les Domingues developed a two-hour crawfish eating contest. A fifteen-minute peeling contest featuring the fastest professional crawfish peelers from the crawfish processing plants vying for the title of "world's fastest crawfish peeler" was also held for the first time.

Organizers brought in other attractions that were non-Cajun but crowd-pleasing just the same. A street fair—local parlance for carnival rides with

Musicians at the 1960 Breaux Bridge Crawfish Festival most likely called their music French music before they began calling it Cajun music. Today, Cajun music and crawfish are almost synonymous. *John S. (Putsie) Angelle.*

midway games—always accompanied the festival and was a moneymaker for the festival association. A U.S. Navy swift boat participated in the boat parade and wowed the crowd with its maneuvers.[249] A Tennessee walking horse exhibition showed Louisiana there were other equines besides its famous quarter horses.[250] A crack squadron of skydivers performed, and National Guard helicopter rope-climbing teams simulated rescue operations.[251]

Once Simon's two-year stint as CFA president was over, he set his sights on maximizing profits for his family's downtown business. Simon knew that many loved traditional Cajun French music, but the people who drank the most beer and ate the most crawfish were the frat boys and sorority girls and the children raised on rock 'n' roll. They saw Elvis Presley's electrifying performance of the song "Crawfish" in the movie *King Creole*.[252] They had been molded by the rock music they heard and saw on *American Bandstand*. Local television stations had afternoon rock-hop TV shows that taught

1964 Breaux Bridge Crawfish Festival officers Ray Pellerin (left) and Carl Simon (right) pose with Crawfish Queen Judy Broussard. *Ashton Roberthon family.*

teenagers, including young Americanized Cajuns, how to rock and have fun.[253] Factoring in Louisiana's young legal drinking age of eighteen, the bandstand crowd in front of Simon's was always larger than the group at Farmers & Merchants Bank.

Simon became the master of the three-day street festival, and there was nothing his customers wanted for in the way of souvenirs, posters, entertainment, drink and food. "The Crawfish Festival became an extended part of my business," Simon said. "I made it what it was, and the day after the festival, we started working on what we were going to do next year. It was business, and it was lucrative because I made it so."[254]

Because the Breaux Bridge downtown was essentially shut down with crowds and traffic from Friday afternoon through Sunday afternoon, merchants could not leave their businesses to go hunting for supplies if they ran out of beer, bread or crawfish.

"I was self-sufficient every year," Simon said. "Crawfish étouffée became our designation. The crawfish dog was easy to do. Every year we'd get better and innovative."[255]

He added frozen margaritas and daiquiris to his repertoire and started a line of souvenir T-shirts. By the 1980s, some of Simon's festival shirts, as well as those of his competitors, were emblazoned with double-entendre messages. "We had this one khaki-colored shirt," said Carleen Simon, a former Jr. Crawfish Queen. "It had a picture of a crawfish and red letters that said 'Eat my tail and suck my head.'"[256]

Downtown space was at a premium, and some merchants rented their space to "carpetbaggers by the square inch,"[257] Simon said. The Simon family—Carl, Renella and daughters Carleen, Liz, Karen, Michelle and Simone—became a well-oiled merchandising machine during the days of the downtown Breaux Bridge Crawfish Festival. As the daughters got older, they recruited college friends to volunteer to work the beer, souvenir, T-shirt, mixed drink and food counters. "They all worked for free because it was a party," Carleen said.[258]

Only once did a usurper out-innovate Carl:

> These carpetbaggers came in, and I'm watching them unload five-gallon cans of cooking oil. They were frying crawfish. Well, they kicked the can all the way up and down the street because you could eat the crawfish while walking down the midway, and people weren't eating my étouffée. They wanted that little fried tail. Next Crawfish Festival, I was in the fried festival food business. I had a thirty-five-pound chicken fryer with the big basket and I had heat lamps to keep 'em warm. The carpetbaggers didn't operate at all against me that next year. But I had to go around and find a fryer.[259]

With upward of fifty thousand tourists crowding the intersection of Bridge and Main Streets, all the downtown merchants who chose to participate experienced a jubilee during the festival.

Breaux Bridge residents enjoyed the attention—for a while. What began as an exuberant celebration of old-timey Cajun life and the culinary blessings of the crawfish was rapidly evolving into an over-the-top street party. Festival organizers limited the big three-day productions of the festival to even-numbered years, and that may be part of the reason why the downtown festival location lasted until 1993.

Simon said he wasn't sure why the "big" festival was held every other year. "I don't know if there was any particular thought behind it, but it was held every other year," Simon said. "That was good…not by design, but it made the locals forget about what they were complaining about."[260]

The complaints included nightmare traffic; loud music; a crowd of drinkers in the street morning, noon and night; and the smell of crawfish shells. "The Crawfish Festival was not very popular locally, but those of us who were in it had fun with it," Simon said.[261]

Older residents, perhaps shocked at the antics of the Woodstock generation they saw on television, began to grumble; 1972 CFA president Robert Les Domingues recognized that the nostalgic themes of the Old South didn't hold much sway with the new visitors. "Back then, French music and dancing, baby contests, crawfish racing, the crowning of the Crawfish Queen and parades of homemade floats were the festival's daily fare," Domingues said, "[but] this is a family picnic, not a rock festival."[262]

Traffic was always a problem. There were five roads into Breaux Bridge, and by end of the festival, traffic was backed up for miles on all of them. Sometimes, visiting dignitaries were advised to park their cars at Ruth Canal on Highway 31 five miles south of town and take a ferry to the bridge.[263]

Picayune writer Howard Jacobs enjoyed writing about Cajuns, a group more comfortable speaking French than English. He sometimes poked fun at their proclivity to fracture the spoken English word. He described a brief conversation between a stranded motorist and a bearded horseman who was easily outpacing cars snarled in a traffic jam. The woman asked for a ride, to which the horseman replied, "*Mais, non!* With all these people on my horse, I couldn't pass!"[264]

In the days before portable toilet rentals were readily available, festival organizers came up with an interesting solution to accommodate the bodily needs of the thousands of beer drinkers. "We removed the manhole covers on the streets and built plywood privies around them," said Ray Pellerin, Crawfish Festival president of 1966.[265]

Other problems surfaced. Catholic Breaux Bridge wanted to attend Mass on Sunday morning, so city officials had to work all night to clean streets littered with thousands of beer cans and pounds of discarded crawfish shells. St. Bernard Cemetery was also abused by revelers who used the aboveground tombs as beds or by lovers looking for privacy.[266] "They played tag in the cemetery, helped themselves to private property and left behind them a trail of food and crawfish wherever they went," Domingues said. "I remember seeing kids necking and making love on the open ground—something no man wants his wife and family subject to."[267]

Other small-town festivals decided to close up shop. Mansura's Cochon de Lait Festival shut down in 1972 because of civil rights issues. Pierre Part hosted a competing crawfish festival, but it closed when it became too large and too rowdy.[268]

New York Times correspondent Roy Reed observed that "the long-standing rites of spring in this area have been discovered by the young from other regions. The young outsiders [are] turning the puritan ethic of their fathers on its head try[ing] to out celebrate the Louisianans. Some of the thousands who come inevitably end up in orgies of drunkenness and destructiveness that appall the residents."[269]

Despite the misgivings, the 1968 Crawfish Festival was the biggest and most successful to date, and a larger "off-year" festival was allowed in 1969. After the 1970 festival, the town hosted three large street parties in a row, and the Louisiana Tourist Commission declared the Breaux Bridge Crawfish Festival the second-largest tourist attraction after the New Orleans Mardi Gras.[270]

Normally, being the second-largest tourist attraction in the state would be good news, and it *was* good news. Area hotels were full, merchants made money, the crawfish industry received free publicity and tourists were learning how to *laissez le bon temps rouler*. The need for Breaux Bridge to secede from the Union had passed.

But questions emerged. How long could the city tolerate the party? How much could the city afford? How many police and emergency workers would be needed to watch over the town's 5,000 residents and 100,000 visitors? Would the city want to continually assume the liability? How would the fire department respond to a major fire during the event?

The festival organizers had a plan. They would purchase a park away from the downtown with ample parking for visitors and campers and large enough to hold the food, merchants, music and street fair. Several properties along the rural part of Rees Street were under consideration.

The park idea was a stroke of genius. Previously, the merchants were making the lion's share of the money. In a downtown festival format, there was no way the CFA could charge admission to the party. The organization made money only on the street fair and ticket sales to the Crawfish Queen Coronation Ball.[271]

The festival association applied to the Evangeline Economic Development District for a $15,000 grant to buy park acreage, but its project was ranked fourth out of five competing projects.[272] The 1970 festival president Aubrey Heumann took quick action and announced at a January 22, 1971 press conference that the 1971 Crawfish Festival was off. He also suggested that if the association was unsuccessful in getting the needed funds for the project, the 1972 festival might be the last.

Was the CFA bluffing? Would it have ended the most successful Louisiana commodity festival in history in a snit over state funding?

The question was never answered because, within a month, the Tourist Commission gave the city $12,481 to buy the land. The town chipped in an additional $5,000, while the festival association provided $10,000—and all of a sudden there was talk of the federal government providing matching funds to build an Acadian Museum, Crawfish Festival building and a camping facility.

In October 1971, the city agreed to buy thirty-five arpents from sugarcane farmer Andrew Hardy for $68,000 over a three-year period. The city would take possession of the land as soon as Hardy's 1971 crop was harvested in December. [273]

The sugarcane harvest came and went, and the city took possession of the land and immediately leveled the blackjack gumbo farmland. The 1972 Crawfish Festival was saved. The downtown merchants reluctantly decided to move their operations to the newly christened Parc Hardy. Town residents would be able to attend Mass on Main Street unmolested, the merchants had first crack at the space reserved for beer and food sales, the festival association would be able to charge a fee for admission and there would be plenty of space for visitors to park. Everyone was a winner.

But weather happens.

In 1959, Bishop Schexnayder bestowed a special papal blessing from Rome upon the city in honor of its centennial, apparently holding off a threatening rain. The centennial was a runaway success. In 1972, one thousand papal blessings wouldn't have been enough to stop the torrential rainstorm that hit Breaux Bridge on the festival's April 28 opening day.[274] The former cane field, just four months removed from harvest, had no time to settle and was reduced to a soupy goo.

The CFA took immediate action. It decided to move the festival back to the downtown area and the front and backgrounds of Breaux Bridge High School.

In a mocking twist of fate, as if an unknown voice was chanting, "Come back to downtown," some fifteen thousand pounds of CFA boiled crawfish, worth $4,000, was lost due to improper icing.[275]

Crawfish Festival spokesman Robert Irwin estimated the crowd at 45,000 to 50,000 (half of the anticipated 100,000),[276] but the show did go on—downtown. And it remained downtown until 1993.

It was another thirteen years before the CFA had the support to return to Parc Hardy.

By the late 1970s, partly because of the success of the Breaux Bridge Crawfish Festival, French-speaking Louisiana had rediscovered its Cajun roots.[277] Cajun everything became cool. Cajun food, especially the crawfish-specializing restaurants of Henderson, boomed when Interstate 10 opened in 1974. Crawfish pond research basics had been firmly established and

Breaux Bridge residents experiencing joie de vivre in the 1974 Crawfish Festival parade. *Grace Amy Irwin.*

pond acreage increased. Cajunism, the "feeling that the Cajun lifestyle was the best way of life," was reaching new heights.[278] So was the Crawfish Festival. The celebration was more popular than ever with the visiting public and a major polarizing controversy among Breaux Bridge residents.

From 1972 to 1984, the official Crawfish Festival events occurred on grounds behind the Breaux Bridge High School and city property along Bayou Teche. The area was cordoned off, and a small admission was charged. The association made money selling beer and boiled crawfish and provided entertainment, but the late-night action remained centered on downtown.

In 1982, Mayor Vance Theriot realized something needed to be done as cleanup charges, portable toilets and police protection costs escalated. The city spent $10,000 in 1980 for those services.[279] At an informal city hall meeting two years later, downtown merchants who reaped festival benefits were asked to donate cash to defray cleanup costs. The only thing decided?

The University Of
Southwestern Louisiana

Aquatic Studies Program

I. Crawfish Depredation In Rice Fields

II. Procedures For Improving Small, Non-commercial
Crawfish Ponds

III. A New Technique For Handling Crawfish Traps

by Donald Gooch

Crawfish Research Center
USL ASP 75 05

Cover of a 1975 University of Louisiana at Lafayette Aquatic Studies Program research booklet on the cultivation of crawfish. *University of Louisiana at Lafayette.*

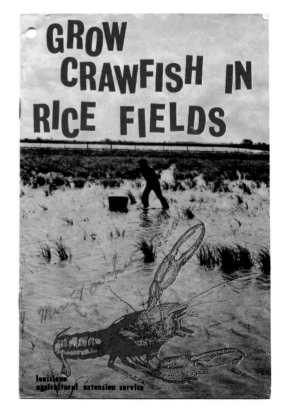

Grow Crawfish in Rice Fields, published in 1963 by the LSU Agricultural Extension Service, was the first publication to suggest that rice farmers could supplement their incomes by double-cropping with crawfish. *Barbara Trahan Broussard/LSU Aquaculture.*

TO PAT HUVAL

CRAWFISH ARE MORE THAN A SPECIALTY!

Yes, the Huvals have spent the greatest part of their adult lives in the preparation of crawfish dishes. Etouffee, Bisque, Boulettes or boiled, there are few, if any, methods of crawfish preparation that they haven't improved on.

Through trial and error in the past they have developed just the right blend of herbs and seasonings that not only complement but improve the delicate crawfish flavor without overpowering it.

The Huvals have reached the peak of perfection in their crawfish dishes and are now using these same seasonings, with minor variations, in all of their seafood offerings.

Crawfish are certainly more than a specialty at Pats but whether you order crawfish, shrimp, oysters or the alien Florida lobster you will be certain to savor the Huvals' cajun touch that has made each famous throughout Louisiana.

Fresh from the bayou.........

Native Louisiana Crawfish, farm grown here in Henderson, are caught daily and rushed to our kitchens. Pat Huval modestly says that the main reason for the popularity of his crawfish dishes is that they are grown right here in Henderson, La., the town where it all began. "No where in the world can the delicate flavor of the Henderson Crawfish be matched." Pat proudly boasts.

To the pot ....

When you combine the Henderson grown Crawfish with the Cajun knowhow of Pat Huval's kitchen staff, the results have to be perfection. Whichever Crawfish dish you order, one thing is certain, it will be the finest Crawfish dish you have ever eaten.

Left: Back cover of menu for Pat's Waterfront Restaurant in Henderson. Pat's could seat more than seven hundred. Add in Robin's, Las's and Charley's Hut restaurants, and Henderson could host nearly three thousand crawfish diners at one sitting. *Pat Huval.*

Below: Onlookers line Bayou Teche for the 1964 Crawfish Festival boat parade and enjoy *Monsieur L'Écrevisse*, designed and built by P.H. LeBlanc, Don Prejean and Breaux Bridge high school students. *Ashton Roberthon family.*

Crawfish peelers dump a tub of crawfish onto a peeling table pre-1968. At many early peeling plants, peelers were responsible for boiling their own crawfish. *LSU Aquaculture.*

Wild crawfish trappers like Walter Angelle of Henderson must travel deep into the Atchafalaya Basin to harvest what used to be called "deepwater" crawfish. *Ron J. Berard.*

Well-seasoned boiled crawfish are sold at Tony's Seafood in Baton Rouge. During peak crawfish season, Tony's employs three off-duty policemen to direct traffic in the parking lot. *Sam Irwin.*

The French Market in New Orleans remains a large market for crawfish, but much of the peeled crawfish used in its recipes is imported from China. Prior to the 1920s, crawfish could be caught within city limits; afterward, fishermen had to travel as far as West End, Gentilly and Kenner. *Sam Irwin.*

Above: Wild crawfish trapper Jody
Meche of Henderson empties a long
crawfish trap onto his sorting table.
Water conditions in the Atchafalaya
Basin vary from year to year and
affect crawfish production. *Sam Irwin*.

Right: Crawfish-adorned Helen
and Pete Drago of Covington,
Louisiana, have visited the Breaux
Bridge Crawfish Festival many
times, serving as parade marshals for
the 2007 festival. *Sam Irwin*.

Above: Barbara Trahan Broussard of Lafayette holds the Trahan's Crayfish Farm sign from father Voorhies Trahan's pond. Trahan's 1949 pond was the first rice/crawfish double-crop farm. *Sam Irwin.*

Left: George Viavant's *Louisiana Crawfish* was painted in 1913. Viavant was inspired by the bayous, marshes and wildlife of the Pelican State. *Roger Houston Ogden Collection.*

Mrs. Charles Hebert of Breaux Bridge owned and operated Main Street's Hebert Hotel in the 1920s and '30s. She and Aline Guidry Champagne share credit for the creation and naming of the crawfish étouffée recipe. *Painting by Elouise Voorhies Gary, Ray Pellerin Collection.*

Live crawfish are first placed on a sorting table on a harvesting boat so that bait and other debris may be removed before sacking the catch. *Sam Irwin.*

Above: Pat Huval of Henderson bought Guidry's Place in 1954 but quickly sold the nightclub/ restaurant to build a restaurant and focus on food. Today, Pat's Fisherman's Wharf is located on the east bank of Bayou Amy. *Sam Irwin*.

Left: Crawfish peelers at Bayou Land Seafood in Cecilia peel crawfish for quality restaurants. Though some local labor is available, many processors use H-2B guest workers for the seasonal work. *Sam Irwin*.

The rare 1984 Crawfish Festival poster issued by the Breaux Bridge Crawfish Festival Merchants Association portrayed Lester "Ta-Tan" Guidry, who built possibly the first commercial crawfish pond. *Christina Kidder*.

A crawfish never leaves his post—he will defend his ground against any threat, including trains and automobiles. However, he will "crawfish" away when he sees a hungry Cajun. *Sam Irwin*.

Above: Sadie Brasseaux, a member of the teen service group called the Ecrevettes, assists during the crawfish-eating contest and other events during the Breaux Bridge Crawfish Festival. *Sam Irwin*.

Top right: Author Sam Irwin enjoys a 2009 Mardi Gras crawfish boil hosted by Jeff Davis Parish crawfish farmer Burt Tietje. Crawfish may be harvested as early as November and as late as July. *Sam Irwin*.

Bottom right: Fresh Louisiana crawfish tail meat in the display case at Tony's Seafood in Baton Rouge. Hand-peeled labor costs and strong demand for live crawfish keep peeled product prices around fourteen dollars per pound. *Sam Irwin*.

Employees handpick "select" crawfish at Tony's Seafood. Merchants began selecting large crawfish for the Swedish market but soon found that the American consumer was willing to pay for large crawfish as well. *Sam Irwin*.

Gilbert's Crawfish Tub rises from the Louisiana rice field prairie in rural Crowley, Acadia Parish. Burt Gilbert began farming crawfish in the late 1950s. Acadia is Louisiana's leading crawfish-producing parish. *Sam Irwin*.

Above: Crawfish Town, USA, is located at the Interstate 10 exit in Henderson, Louisiana. Improved transportation in the 1930s helped to create the crawfish market. When I-10 opened in 1973, crawfish restaurants in Henderson boomed. *Ron J. Berard*.

Right: Breaux Bridge crawfish farmer Mike Clay examines some of his catch. St. Martin Parish produces farm-raised crawfish from ponds and wild crawfish from the Atchafalaya Basin. *Sam Irwin*.

The bridge over Bayou Amy pays tribute to the town's crawfish heritage. Louisiana's Highway 352 terminates at the foot of the West Atchafalaya River Protection Levee. *Sam Irwin*.

The Crawfish Races, created by early Breaux Bridge Crawfish Festival organizer Woody Marshall, remains a popular event. Famed Kentucky Derby announcer Heywood Hale Broun called the race during the 1974 festival. *Sam Irwin*.

Above: The image of the crawfish is ubiquitous in south Louisiana and has come to represent both Cajun culture and the state. *Sam Irwin*.

Left: The Breaux Bridge telephone directory featured a crawfish on its cover during the 1960s. The crawfish image appeared on the phone book in various forms until 1974. *Reprinted with permission of CenturyLink Inc.*

Attend the Church of
Your Choice. See the
YELLOW PAGES for
Church Addresses

Breaux Bridge
Arnaudville, Cecilia,
Henderson, Parks
Telephone Directory

Find Us Fast
In The
Yellow Pages

JULY, 1966

Right: Jeff Davis Parish crawfish farmer Burt Tietje conducts an ecotour of his crawfish pond for travel writers in 2009. The Jeff Davis Parish Tourist Commission schedules the tour on a seasonal basis. *Sam Irwin*.

Below: Crawfish pond acreage in Louisiana. *LSU Aquaculture*.

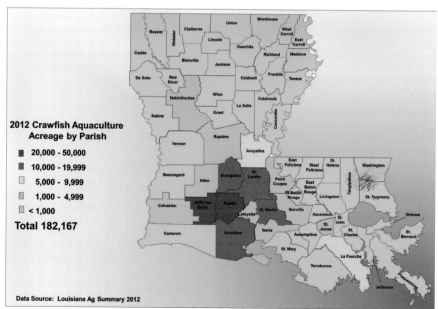

2012 Crawfish Aquaculture Acreage by Parish

■ 20,000 - 50,000
■ 10,000 - 19,999
□ 5,000 - 9,999
▨ 1,000 - 4,999
□ < 1,000

Total 182,167

Data Source: Louisiana Ag Summary 2012

Firmin Breaux's bridge eventually became a drawbridge that frequently opened for oil barge traffic from the Anse La Butte oil field west of Breaux Bridge. The crawfish is the symbol of the city. *Ron J. Berard.*

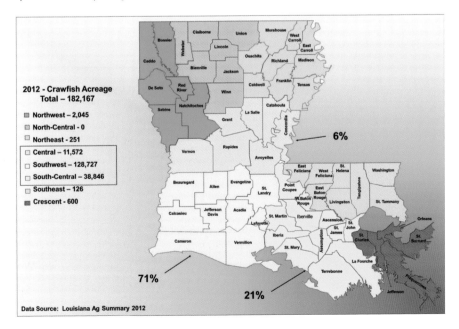

2012 - Crawfish Acreage
Total – 182,167

- Northwest – 2,045
- North-Central - 0
- Northeast - 251
- Central – 11,572
- Southwest – 128,727
- South-Central – 38,846
- Southeast – 126
- Crescent - 600

6%

71%

21%

Data Source: Louisiana Ag Summary 2012

Southwest Louisiana became the leading crawfish supplier in the 1980s, when rice prices dipped and farmers realized they could make money with the crustacean. *LSU AgCenter.*

The merchants set a uniform price for festival beer. Glass containers were also banned.[280]

The *Teche News* festival-reporting headline was markedly different from past coverage. Instead of "Thousands Attend Fest," the header was ominous. "Breaux Bridge Recovering from Festival Invasion" implied an inconvenience, almost a nuisance, for the city.[281] Most residents said the 1982 festival was the largest yet, and some estimated the crowd at 150,000 to 200,000.

Festival president Rudy Raggio calculated that sixteen thousand pounds of boiled crawfish had been consumed on the festival grounds and at least that much had been eaten by the downtown crowds. The beer flowed freely.[282] Despite the large crowds, no calamity to the town or to visitors ever occurred during the Crawfish Festival, a remarkable feat considering how much alcohol was consumed.[283]

Downtown merchants were now responsible for providing their own musical entertainments, and Carl Simon had a reputation for having the best bands and the widest variety of refreshments.[284] Simon could read the writing on the wall. He knew there was a group that wanted to end the downtown bacchanal and return it to the slowly developing Parc Hardy on the outskirts of town. The CFA was gaining public support by pushing the idea of building a civic center at the park and improving the grounds. Simon knew he would have to gather his forces for battle, and he and his brother, Chester Lee Simon, a longtime local politico, supported city council candidates who supported the Simons. The Simons always had the three votes they needed on the five-man city council:

> *They* [the anti-downtown festival group] *became challenging, and I had trouble getting votes, but I always had three councilmen. They kept the pressure on the councilmen. In 1984, they went to the city and demanded that we not have a festival. So the city said, "Y'all appoint a committee, three on each side, and y'all have meetings. Y'all resolve it yourselves." We had meetings, but there was no budging. We went back to the city without a resolution. City Councilman Johnny Martin was pro-festival, and he brought it up to a vote, and the council gave us a permit to have a one-day festival on Saturday. It took all the ingenuity and savvy I could pull. We didn't have the parade, but we had everything that looked like a festival. All you need is beer, music and people. You had Mim's Restaurant, Theresa's Restaurant, Lloyd Tauzin at the bridge. So we pulled it off.*[285]

In 1984, CFA president Russell "Shorty" Huval said the organization would have nothing to do with the scaled-down event. "There is no way we are going to endorse anything of that sort," Huval said. But he was not against the black residents represented by the Crustacean Association, which held its crawfish festival on the southwest side of town. "They have never disrupted the community. There is no reason they could not hold the *fais do-do* at the time the festival is going on in Parc Hardy,"[286] Huval said.

Huval also said the CFA was unfairly blamed for the excesses of the downtown crowds. "Those activities have never been part of the festival staged by us. We have never received any monies from it and accept no blame,"[287] he said.

As a result of the council's vote, the CFA excused itself from the festival as the newly formed Breaux Bridge Crawfish Festival Merchants Association, commonly called the "Downtown Merchants," hosted an abbreviated crawfish festival.[288]

Another issue arose from the decision by the CFA to withdraw from the party. The CFA began the tradition of sponsoring an official festival poster in 1978 and generated some benefit from the sales of the artwork. Resident Virginia Yongue partnered with local artist Caroline Dupuy to create and market the first official Crawfish Festival poster. Dupuy produced many posters for the CFA, but in 1984, the *Morning Advocate* ran an announcement in "Art Notes" that Baton Rouge artist Alan Laurie "is the artist of the 1984 Crawfish Festival poster, a six-color silk-screened limited edition depicting a happy man devouring crawfish."[289] CFA records indicate that Dupuy's poster was the official poster, but that didn't stop Laurie or the Downtown Merchants Association from offering art capitalizing on the Crawfish Festival theme.[290]

The merchants' poster was a striking depiction of Lester "Ta-Tan" Guidry, a crawfish farmer who may have built the first crawfish pond in the state. The art, created by Christina Kidder, portrays the elderly Guidry, his face leathered by years of outdoor work, lifting a crawfish trap from the water.[291] Other well-known Louisiana artists whose designs were chosen to officially represent the Crawfish Festival include Elemore Morgan Jr., Kelly Guidry, Richard "Dickie" Landry, Francis X. Pavy and Tony Bernard.[292]

By 1986, the CFA returned to the party fold but moved all of its activities to Parc Hardy. The preview article that ran in Baton Rouge's *State Times* was penned by *Teche News* feature writer Gladys DeVillier. DeVillier, surely familiar with the controversies surrounding the Crawfish Festival, made no mention of the 1984 unpleasantness between the rival factions. She merely listed the activities sponsored by all three festival organizations: the Breaux Bridge CFA, the Downtown Merchants and the Crustacean Association.[293]

The CFA had the two hottest bands in the area, Grammy Award winner Rockin' Sidney of "Don't Mess with My Toot Toot" fame and college favorite Atchafalaya. The Downtown Merchants had eight music stages and twenty bands, including Beausoleil and Zachary Richard.[294] DeVillier's article also gave festivalgoers two hotline numbers—Simon's Pharmacy and the CFA office—to call for information.

The major difference between the two locations was that Parc Hardy activities shut down at 1:00 a.m. on Friday and midnight on Saturday. Downtown partied until bar-closing time, which was 2:00 a.m.[295]

The CFA's theme, "Vive Notre Heritage" (Our Heritage Lives), remained true to the established traditions of past festivals. In lieu of a Catholic Mass, a crawfish harvest blessing was conducted, and a good old-fashioned Cajun cracklin' cook-off was launched. The Downtown Merchants featured a beefcake Mr. Crawfish contest, its qualifications based strictly on "looks and physique."[296] A Seattle visitor to the Bayou State noted that "eating crayfish in Seattle is a religious ceremony, while eating crawfish in Louisiana is a pagan ritual."[297]

Breaux Bridge residents continued the newly established tradition of wearing nineteenth-century garb to celebrate the 1960 Crawfish Festival. *Joseph S. (Putsie) Angelle.*

Traffic was gridlocked for much of the weekend because Breaux Bridge was now hosting three separate festivals: one in Parc Hardy on the north side, one near the National Guard Armory Hall on the south side and one in the downtown center. And now the massive traffic jams would occur every year instead of every other year because the city council granted permits to hold the festival annually.

Attendance figures varied widely for the festivals in the late '80s and early '90s. Some estimates were as high as 300,000.[298] Something had to give. Old stalwarts like Mayor Louis Kern, who had returned to civic duty after a hiatus, realized that the Crawfish Festival had gotten too big. "It's too much for a town of 7,000," Kern said in 1990. "This time it was unreal."[299]

The city had long relied on help from other law enforcement agencies, including the St. Martin, Iberia and Lafayette sheriff's offices and the state police, to help secure the city, but the mayor and Police Chief George Menard were constantly worried that emergency vehicles would not be able to get through if a fire or some other serious emergency occurred. "We've been blessed that we haven't had any serious problems in all these years," Menard said.[300]

Finally, the crawfish pot boiled over for the Downtown Merchants in 1992 when Mayor Kern appointed a twelve-member Crawfish Festival Advisory Commission to come up with recommendations for the festival. The advisory group held eight informational meetings and eight public hearings. It recommended new rules and regulations for the festival, chief among them the elimination of the downtown festival. The group reported to a three-member Crawfish Festival Commission, which reviewed the recommended changes.[301] The Crawfish Festival Commission members were Councilman Kenneth LeBlanc, CFA president Calvin LaGrange and Wallace Williams of the Creole Festival Association. The city council held two "no-holds barred" public hearings[302] in which many harsh words were spoken.[303] At stake were the windfall profits that benefitted the downtown merchants when 100,000 thirsty and hungry visitors descended on the city and the peace of mind of the town's 7,000 residents.

Even the Protestants of Breaux Bridge, a heretofore marginal group on the subject of the Crawfish Festival, banded together and let their feelings be known. "They organized and came en masse to one of the hearings and said they were against selling beer in the street," said Ray Pellerin. "That didn't go over too well."[304]

But Carl Simon knew the time had come. The city council approved most of the recommendations made by the advisory commission, which ended the downtown party.

"I had support on the council, but when [St. Martin Parish] Sheriff Charles Fuselier said, 'If the festival is held downtown, I ain't coming,' that was it," Simon said.[305]

The city council voted 3–2 to ban all downtown crawfish festival activities but allowed the Creole Festival Association to continue its festival on North Bridge Street near the National Guard Armory.[306] The party, at least at the intersection of Bridge and Main, was over. The lights were turned out.

A petition calling for the reinstitution of the downtown festival was subsequently circulated and drew two thousand signatures. "Never in the history of Louisiana has a town ever destroyed its own attraction. My feet want to be back on the street," read the petition,[307] but it didn't sway the council's mind.

Visiting partygoers who did not get the news and arrived at Bridge and Main Street for 1993's bacchanal were briefly confused and firmly directed to Parc Hardy by the many police officers patrolling Breaux Bridge's downtown. The officers also strictly enforced the town's new open container law that banned consumption of adult beverages on the street.[308]

But for the first time in thirty-three years during a Crawfish Festival weekend, a funeral could be conducted at St. Bernard Catholic Church because there was no downtown crowd partying in the streets. *Teche News* publisher Henri C. Bienvenu noted the following in his May 5 "Pense Donc!!" column:

> *For the first time in years homeowners felt completely secure within their houses and their property and were able to come and go pretty much at will. There was even a funeral at St. Bernard Saturday morning, an event that would not have been possible on any festival weekend over the past 30 or so years.*
>
> *Volunteer firemen were called out twice over the weekend and had no trouble responding to the alarms. Downtown traffic, while a bit congested for a few brief interludes, moved freely throughout the three days. For a change law enforcement officials appeared to be in complete control of the situation.*
>
> *On the other end of the opinion spectrum, those downtown merchants who were able to reap enormous profits during previous festivals are naturally upset and resentful that their golden goose has pretty much been killed.*[309]

One other controversy was resolved in 2005 when Mayor Jack Dale Delhomme, backed by the city council, ended the African American version of the crawfish festival.

Under the social customs of the 1950s and '60s, the African Americans of Breaux Bridge staged a separate crawfish festival that attracted even more tourists to the city. The black citizenry put on a parade, chose a queen and generally had a good street party on Bridge Street near the National Guard Armory Hall. The organizing group had changed over the years. At one time, it was the Crustacea Crawfish Festival Association and, later, the Creole Crawfish Festival Association.[310] In 2005, the sponsoring group was called the Afro-American Crawfish Association.

Trouble was on the horizon for the group in 2004, when the city council refused to help fund the black celebration. Dave Thibodeaux, president of the Afro-American Association, said the city had always paid the upfront costs for both festivals, but Mayor Delhomme said the black organization had not paid the city back in "10 or 12" years.[311] The plan was to stop funding for the black festival for one year, a proposal that even the black councilmen could get behind.

However, the following year, the city council required both festivals to pay in advance for police and security. The Afro-American Crawfish Festival couldn't come up with the $15,000 required. At the March 2, 2005 council meeting, Councilman Kenneth LeBlanc suggested that the city "needed only one crawfish festival."[312] Faster than a professional crawfish peeler could peel *Monsieur Écrevisse*, a motion was put on the floor and the council voted to sponsor only one festival, the one organized by the CFA.[313]

The vote was on racial lines, but everyone agreed the real issue was money. City money was tight, and Mayor Delhomme said it was a "burden on the city that we would have to put up the money for security."[314]

There was grumbling from black residents, but no one could argue against municipal fiscal restraint. Besides, Delhomme argued, having separate festivals sent out the wrong message to the rest of the world. "We are the only city in America that has segregated festivals," Delhomme said. "It's time for it to stop."[315]

Would the crawfish industry have grown from 200,000 pounds in 1959 to 126 million pounds by 2012 without the Crawfish Festival? Maybe. However, there is no other single entity more responsible for the success of the crawfish industry than the Crawfish Festival and residents of Breaux Bridge.

Early scientific researchers noted that the reason for their research was because "promotional efforts such as the Crawfish Festival have increased the demand for crawfish and have generated greater interest in their production."[316]

The national media continues to report from the bayou town. The *New York Times*, *Wall Street Journal*, *Grit*, *National Geographic*, *Southern Living*, *Better*

Homes and Gardens, *Maxim*, *Country Cooking*, *Motorhome Living*, *USA Today*, ABC, CBS, NBC, CNN, PBS, the Food Channel and hundreds of other media sources have all reported on the banks of Bayou Teche "from Breaux Bridge, where the crawfish is king."[317]

Trade groups organized: the Louisiana Crawfish Industry Development Association in 1965,[318] the Louisiana Crawfish Farmers Association in 1970,[319] the Louisiana Crawfish Producers Association in 1983,[320] the Louisiana Crawfish Promotion and Research Board in 1983 and the Associated Crawfish Processors of Louisiana in 1984.[321] But those groups have never been able to attract anything near the numbers of the Crawfish Festival. The first crawfish trade show didn't even take place until 1984.[322]

Then there are the numbers. The lowest crowd estimates for festival attendance were in 1959, when the *Picayune* said 20,000 enjoyed crawfish in Breaux Bridge. The *Advocate* had the figure at 70,000. The highest estimates were in the range of 300,000, but 1966 CFA president Ray Pellerin disputed the larger numbers. "We looked at aerial photographs," Pellerin said. "And if you allocate four feet per person, there's no way the numbers could be that high; 100,000 people was about it."[323]

The most frequent attendance number cited through the years was 100,000, so arithmetic tells the tale—100,000 visitors to Breaux Bridge for fifty-five

Today's Breaux Bridge Crawfish Festival features French Louisiana music and attracts internationally known Cajun musicians like Balfa Toujours. *Sam Irwin.*

Crawfish Festivals means 5.5 million people visited Breaux Bridge during the celebration. Corporate research reports that 33 percent of satisfied customers recommend good services to their friends.[324] That means the Breaux Bridge Crawfish Festival, winner of multiple Louisiana Food and Fairs Festival of the Year awards, is sure to expect many more first-time visitors.

Mayor Louis Kern believes the reason for Breaux Bridge's success as a town and the crawfish capital is in the water. "There's an old saying," he said. "*Celui qui boit l'eau du Bayou Tèche va certainement revenir.* He who drinks the water of the Teche will certainly return."[325]

CHAPTER 7

CRAWFISH RANCHING

For biologist Percy Viosca, the catfish dinner at Robin's Seafood House alone was worth the trip to the west side of the Atchafalaya Basin. He had often visited Pierre Part, Bayou Pigeon and Bayou Sorrel on the eastern side of the basin and written about their crawfish culture. In 1950, Viosca championed the crawfish as the only natural enemy of the invasive water hyacinth. "If it were not for these swamp creatures…our waters would be completely covered over with [water hyacinths].[326]

Viosca also mentioned in his 1949 "Crawfish to the Rescue" article for the *Times-Picayune New Orleans States* magazine that crawfish served as a food source for commercially valuable Atchafalaya species like fish, turtles and bullfrogs. In almost an afterthought, Viosca noted that crawfish could also "serve…directly as human food."[327]

The following year, "The Super Crawfish from Pierre Part" was featured on the cover of the *Dixie, Times-Picayune-States Roto* magazine.[328] Maybe New Orleanians stopped worrying about their drained crawfish habitats when Viosca promised there was "something new at last in Crayfish Town—crayfish trapping."[329] He noted that there were many "Crayfish Towns" in Louisiana, including Pierre Part and Bayou Sorrel, and mentioned that a "remarkable feature of deepwater crayfish is their large size. This may be due to the greater amount of oxygen and food in the flowing water and their less crowded condition."[330]

As Viosca studied the basin's environmental conditions for the next ten years, he realized that water conditions were constantly changing and affecting crawfish production. He discounted the numerous theories (water temperature too cold, water bird predation, insecticide runoff, overfishing) offered by the crawfish stakeholders for the poor 1959 catch.[331] Instead, he blamed the "polwog catfish" (yellow bullhead), which were abundant during the crawfish hatching season of September and October due to abnormally high water levels.[332] He told the New Iberia Kiwanis Club that "water in the Atchafalaya Swamps usually goes down during the summer, allowing crawfish to dig small caves in which to protect themselves when the swamp water rises. The water did not go down, the crawfish could not build their caves and, as a result, catfish sucked up the crawfish before they could repopulate."[333] He also announced to the Kiwanis that the state was going to farm crawfish in order to study their habitat.

After a lifetime of studying crawfish and other aquatic animals, Viosca must have felt deep satisfaction when he saw bulldozers break ground for the crawfish research pond near Cecilia. He would now have a chance to prove crawfish theories he had been promoting as far back as 1923, when he predicted that the decapod could be cultivated in a farmed environment.[334] There would then be no need, Viosca postulated, to develop crawfish farms unless all the swamps, ponds and ditches of Louisiana became dried up through drainage. All the canals and swamps in Louisiana will likely never be drained, but in 1959, enough of them had been turned into New Orleans lakefront neighborhoods and sugarcane fields that it was a little less convenient for the urban crawfisherman to catch his own.

Viosca told *Picayune* society columnist Howard Jacobs in 1960 that a "crawfish renaissance is under way, thanks to the happy circumstances that more and more folks are going into crawfish cultivation."[335] Viosca had visited the folks who were "going into crawfish cultivation" and was gathering data that he would apply to his research pond. He theorized that the duck hunting leases near the Bayou Teche town of Jeanerette in Iberia Parish were a good location because the "tidal flow has been blocked, thus preventing the influx of natural enemies of crawfish."[336]

Viosca observed aquatic ecology, but other amateur naturalists like Lester "Ta-Tan" Guidry of Breaux Bridge had also spent a lifetime studying the Atchafalaya. Guidry and others like him had worked and lived near the basin and knew how every U.S. Army Corps of Engineers basin flood-control adjustment affected the environment.

Kirby Guidry, the son of Lester Guidry, said in a 2013 interview that his father was a commercial fisherman and carpenter. In the 1930s, for fifty cents a day, his father worked as a laborer building the West Atchafalaya

Protection Levee. "My daddy only had a third-grade education, but he was a naturalist with a vision," Kirby said. "When I was in the Marine Corps, I bought a set of *Encyclopedia Britannica* and sent them home from overseas. When I got home, Daddy had read the entire set."[337]

Kirby said his father was self-educated with an insatiable natural curiosity: "When he brought the researchers to his pond, he identified ten or twelve different species of crawfish."[338]

Lester Guidry also knew that growing crawfish in a controlled environment was possible because he had been doing it for years. Guidry's pond was one of sixteen commercial ponds Viosca studied in 1960 as plans for the research pond were developed.[339]

Breaux Bridge locals consider Guidry's pond to be the first commercial crawfish pond in Louisiana. It may or may not be the "first crawfish pond," but it is logical to assume that the first aquaculture farms would be located in the areas where the crawfish restaurant trade was developing, namely Henderson, Breaux Bridge and Lafayette. Viosca wrote in his "Mudbug Farming" article in the March 1961 *Louisiana Conservationist* that two thousand acres of "crawfish farms…located mostly west of the Atchafalaya floodway" had a production potential of 2 million pounds annually.[340]

Guidry built a 630-acre pond on marginal agricultural land known ominously as Section 28. Technically, Section 28 is the geophysical number assigned to a salt dome oil and natural gas tract east of the village of Parks in St. Martin Parish. Locals often refer to the entire six-mile-long swampy area south of Henderson down to Catahoula as Section 28. "Way out by Section 28" was a phrase that truly meant *le fin fond de tonnèrre* (the end of thunder), aka "the sticks."

Guidry enlisted the aid of "Balon" Guilbeaux and future crawfish entrepreneur Emile Barras of Catahoula, who owned the heavy equipment used to build the levees around the bottomland hardwood lowland naturally populated with crawfish.[341] "The first day the pond was ready, about forty fishermen showed up with dip nets," Kirby said. "Daddy had to stop the fishing because they had caught eighteen thousand pounds by eleven o'clock using those old-fashioned nets."[342]

Guidry's image appeared on the 1984 souvenir poster issued by the Breaux Bridge Crawfish Festival Merchants Association honoring his pioneering efforts in crawfish farming.

Ashby Landry, the creative marketer of Don's Seafood and Steakhouse, drew a lot of attention to crawfish by flamboyantly calling his Henderson crawfish pond a "ranch." Don's Crawfish Ranch received publicity in the

The crawfishermen of Don's Crawfish Ranch used pirogues to navigate the shallow water of the flooded woodland crawfish pond. *Don's Seafood and Steakhouse.*

Morning Advocate, but the Landry brothers also had to buy peeled crawfish from other sources simply because it was quickly developing a mass appeal at their other restaurants.[343] The term "ranching" never took off, but Landry was able to generate a lot of PR mileage with the fanciful idea.

As the crow flies, Guidry's pond and Landry's crawfish ranch were located about forty miles north of Viosca's ideal farm location, namely the Jeanerette area, but Guidry's pond and others proved that crawfish culture could be installed on a variety of land and soil types. Viosca wrote in "Mudbug Farming" that crawfish farming might be a solution for land developers who needlessly drained land in hopes of attracting real estate agents, giving new meaning to the phrase, "I got fifty acres of swampland I want to sell you":

> [Some] *existing crawfish farms…are in alluvial lands where both front lands and back lands, or a combination of the two, are utilized. A number are in the prairie soils of southwestern Louisiana irrigation reservoirs and rice fields proper. Some are in drained wooded swamp, others in so-called reclaimed marshland, dead-end products of the drainage craze which have been waiting for real estate agents who never showed up. Crawfish culture may salvage many of those lost acres.*[344]

Many of the early crawfish farms were conveniently located near swamp-side peeling plants, and economic studies were conducted to help peeling business operators know exactly what the numbers were. Economic research through LSU's College of Food Science and Technology and Agricultural Economics and Agribusiness departments was done to help processors achieve the highest efficiencies.

In 1966, there were thirty-three crawfish-peeling plants in operation. Twenty-two of the processing plants were in Breaux Bridge, Henderson, St. Martinville, Catahoula and New Iberia. On the eastern side of the Atchafalaya Basin, seven crawfish merchants were in business; three were in the rice prairie parishes and one each in Rapides and Avoyelles Parish.[345]

The problem associated with peeling crawfish is that there is a lot of labor and expense to retrieve the tail meat; only 14 percent of the crawfish is a marketable product.[346] According to the *Profitability of Crawfish Peeling Plants in Louisiana* report of 1970 by James F. Hudson and Wildon J. Fontenot, "for a plant owner to obtain one pound of meat, he has to handle approximately seven pounds of whole crawfish. Consequently, the cost of one pound of meat is approximately seven times the price of live crawfish, plus the cost of peeling and delivering."[347]

The University of Louisiana at Lafayette concentrated research on processing, packaging and freezing crawfish and recipe development.[348] Establishment of the crawfish's "keeping qualities" and its chemical composition was crucial to the basic development of the market, and the U.S. Economic Development Administration funded an LSU study to identify the nutritional value of crawfish, chemical composition and rate of bacteria spoilage growth, all critical items affecting processing and packaging.[349]

For the market to grow, peeling plants needed a reliable source of crawfish, and Viosca was intrigued with the notion that crawfish could be rotated with rice, a profitable cash crop for many Louisiana farmers. Catching crawfish in rice fields was common in the Vermilion Parish area. The *Beaumont Enterprise* noted in 1935 that crawfishing was a "primary occupation from two to four months of the year" in the rice country of Abbeville and Bayou Queue de Tortue (Turtle-Tail Bayou),[350] but Viosca named Voorhies Trahan (*traw-hawhn*) of the Ridge community in Lafayette Parish as the first to double-crop rice and crawfish in 1949.[351] "Credit for this development must be given to one Voorhies Trahan, a full-blooded Cajun whose rice fields are located five miles south of Duson [*doo-sawhn*], Louisiana," wrote Viosca. "Although Trahan has had no formal education whatsoever and does not know how to read or write, he is a keen observer of things biological."[352]

Charles Clause of Carencro, Louisiana, uses a washtub and a four-sided "lift" net to catch crawfish in the Voorhies Trahan pond in Judice. Lift nets could be purchased at nearly every general goods store in south Louisiana. *Edward J. Trahan.*

Trahan was netting thirty dollars per acre mono-cropping with rice; with crawfish, he increased his profit up to ninety dollars per acre per year even though his "royalty" was only ten cents a pound.[353]

Barbara Trahan Broussard, Trahan's daughter, said she remembers overhearing conversations her father had with his brothers that date the crawfish/rice rotation to the mid-1940s.[354] "He would flood his fields and let family go get crawfish," Broussard said. "That's how it was at first. In the later '40s, he actually started selling. He had a large family—I was just one of his thirteen kids—so he had more help then to actually catch the crop and sell it to people who were asking for some."[355]

Bait and trapping techniques were worked out on a trial-and-error basis and done with minimum investment at first, Broussard said. Her older half sisters would wade out into the twelve- to eighteen-inch-deep water with a string tied to a corncob and a *carrelet*. As the crawfish flocked to the food, the string would be gently reeled in, and the *carrelet* would be slipped underneath and net the catch.[356]

Aloncel Credeur Trahan, the wife of pioneer rice/crawfish farmer Voorhies Trahan, weighs a sack of crawfish trapped by one of her customers. *Edward J. Trahan.*

Large farming families were the norm in Catholic Louisiana, and children had to help feed the family in whatever way possible. But Broussard noted that when her older sisters married and moved away, her father opened his crawfish farm to the general public to harvest his crop.[357]

Trahan died in 1963, but the rice/crawfish crop rotation continued to operate under the guidance of his widow, Aloncel Credeur Trahan. Aloncel's career as a crawfish farmer was nearly cut short. Still grieving the loss of her husband and worried that holding the water in her rice fields was too much of an expense, she cut holes in the levees to drain the pond. Barbara recalled:

> She was letting water out, but just in case there were a few crawfish to salvage, they had taken large cages with two by fours and cage wire and placed them along the cuts. A neighbor comes by and says, "Miss Trahan, you know that your cages are boiling over with crawfish and there's some crawfish going into the road?" It's true—the cages were flowing over with crawfish, and they were crossing over the ditch and trying to cross over the road into the highway.[358]

Broussard said 1963 turned out to be a bumper-crop year for their pond.[359]

Viosca sent out a census survey in 1961 to gather information on crawfish culture through country agents and soil conservation personnel, and more than two hundred people asked the Louisiana Wildlife and Fisheries Commission for information on crawfish culture.[360] He made contact and advised them on predator control and water supply.[361]

The news of Viosca's research pond was welcomed by everyone, especially the media. Crawfish were always good for a story, but the research pond was big news and covered by the large dailies and smaller weeklies. "South Louisiana's morale last spring was lower than the muddy bottom of Bayou Teche," wrote Jim Levy of Baton Rouge's *Morning Advocate*. "The wild doings of Cuban rebel leader Fidel Castro did not necessarily depress the thousands of Louisiana Cajuns. Cold War talk and school integration in Virginia caused only a small stir. Even the visit of Khrushchev failed to arouse a great deal of interest. It was the crawfish. Or rather, the lack of them. President Eisenhower did not declare south Louisiana a disaster area, but the State Legislature did see fit to set aside $10,000 for study of the grave situation."[362]

Dixie magazine, the *Picayune*'s Sunday supplement, reported that the research pond, located on property owned by George Dupuis near Cecilia's Grand Anse community, was composed of three half-acre sections. One plot was a rice field type with a flat bottom and constant water supply. Another was based on a sugarcane field with mounds rising from the water to emulate the top of high sugarcane rows. The third section had three mounds and four trenches to simulate deeper water and protection from cold water. The plots were fertilized and planted with "delta duck potato" as a food source.[363]

Ruby Trahan, Edward Trahan Jr. and Mr. and Mrs. Charles Clause and their catch at the Voorhies Trahan crawfish pond. Voorhies Trahan allowed the public to fish for a fee. *Edward J. Trahan.*

Viosca thought the trenched pond would produce a better quality of pond crawfish to compete with the "deepwater" crawfish of the Atchafalaya Basin. At the time, it took eight pounds of basin crawfish to produce one pound of meat and ten to twelve pounds of the pond variety to produce the same.[364]

The *Advocate*'s Levy reported that the 250 crawfishermen in the Henderson area often caught four hundred to seven hundred pounds of crawfish on "a run" and that "at 15 cents a pound, that's good money." He added that crawfishermen could gross as much as $3,150 during a ten-week season.[365] Tail meat was wholesaled at $4 a pound.[366]

Restaurateur Pat Huval said the market was roughly divided geographically. "We [west side] buyers don't take care of the New Orleans business," Huval said. "That end is covered by the fishermen in Pierre Part, in Assumption Parish on the East Atchafalaya spillway."[367]

The best Henderson buyers included Huval, Joe Amy, Freddie Zerangue and Bert Montet, Levy said. "In recent years, fishermen haven't had to worry about a market for their precious cargo. Some 15 buyers are in the Henderson area alone," he wrote.[368]

Local residents received their printed news of the crawfish pond from J.S. Badon, the Breaux Bridge correspondent to the *Teche News*, who provided a simplistic report. "[Jesse] Guidry, Cecilia civic leader and caretaker of the Crawfish Experimental Farm at Cecilia, says that the farm is doing nicely," wrote Badon dryly on April 7. "Sample crawfish from the pond were sent to biologists in New Orleans for study."[369]

In 1961, Viosca became the go-to crawfish man for *Picayune* columnist Howard Jacobs and his annual crawfish season prediction story. "Viosca contends that from an economic point of view the crawdad is really the Louisiana caviar," wrote Jacobs in March 1961. "We salute the lobster of the bayous and personally pledge to do away with several hundred portions ere the season is over."[370]

Viosca's tenure in the "Remoulade" column was short-lived. He died on August 28, living just long enough to harvest two crops from the experimental farm. He never had the opportunity to publish anything more than the general "Mudbug Farming" article.[371] "When I have so much knowledge of the fauna and flora, why should this cancer snuff out my life," Viosca asked a fellow scientist.[372]

Crawfish entrepreneurs took advantage of the knowledge base of the managers of the sixteen crawfish ponds Viosca visited in 1960. There were only 2,000 acres of crawfish ponds when Viosca's pilot was built. By the mid-'60s, crawfish farming had increased to more than 7,000 acres.[373] In 2011, there were more than 189,860 acres of land in Louisiana devoted to crawfish aquaculture.[374]

Viosca's crawfish work was under the Louisiana Department of Wildlife and Fisheries, but other agencies provided early opportunities for the budding crawfish industry. The field of astacology was wide open.

Carl Thomas, a biologist with the Soil Conservation Service, conducted crawfish/rice field research on Acadia Parish rice farms owned by Burt Gilbert and Roland Faulk. His 1965 *Preliminary Report on the Agricultural Production of the Red-Swamp in Louisiana Rice Fields* may have been the first published field scientific study related to crawfish aquaculture in Louisiana.[375] Thomas delivered his research report to the Southeastern Association of Game and Fish Commissioners conference.

It didn't take long to figure out that rice could double-crop with crawfish. Farmers plant rice in the spring and then flood-irrigate their fields with water. In late summer, the levees are opened and the water drained. When the fields dried, harvesters were brought in to cut the rice. The field was covered with post-harvest straw and chaff left in the field until the following planting season. Until a crawfish market developed, most rice fields either lay dormant or were flooded with water for duck-hunting activities.[376]

Farmer Roland Faulk, now eighty-three years old, said rice-farming techniques were different in the 1950s and 1960s because rice varieties and tractors were different. Faulk noticed that crawfish naturally occurred in his fields.[377] "Dad used to keep water on the field to rot the [leftover] rice so that during the spring, we could plow easier," Faulk said. "We tried mowing, but that's expensive and time consuming. You'd have to spread out the straw in order to mow. You began your rice season as soon as you could get back into the fields."[378]

Sometime in the '50s, Faulk said his family was invited to the home of his cousin Burt Gilbert, a neighbor who lived a half mile away. "They were having a crawfish boil, and Burt said he thought he could sell some," Faulk said. "Burt just stopped up some water [in a rice field] at the back of his house and saw the crawfish that went in."[379]

Later that year, as Faulk was starting up a well to pump water onto their land, a man drove up and asked if he could go into his field and catch crawfish. "He filled up two big sackfuls," Faulk said. "He had them on the trunk of his car. He said, 'Here's five dollars,' but I said no, that we were going to cut off the water anyway. I guess he had more inside, maybe two hundred or three hundred pounds, and that's when I got the idea of selling crawfish."[380]

Faulk said that within three years, the field set aside for crawfish soon produced enough to fill the demand for the area.[381] "We were making more crawfish than we could really sell, and that's when I went down to Henderson and talked to Mr. [Joe] Amy."[382]

Faulk said he wasn't really concerned with the scientific aspects of crawfish cultivation because the crawfish were just "there," but Thomas got a permit to shoot ducks out of season. "We'd split them open, you know, to see if the ducks were eating the crawfish."[383]

Robert Romaire, the former head of the LSU Aquaculture Research Station within the LSU AgCenter, said James Gerald Broom's 1961 Auburn University master's thesis, "Production of the Louisiana Red Swamp Crawfish *Procambarus clarkii* (Girard) in Ponds," was the first aquaculture study of red swamp crawfish.[384] Broom also wrote a 1963 article for the *Louisiana Conservationist* titled "Natural and Domestic Production of Crawfish," in which he acknowledged that the Atchafalaya Basin was the major source for crawfish but also made a compelling case for research:

> *The crawfish season may vary widely from year to year. In 1958, the Louisiana commercial catch was over two million pounds and in 1959 only two hundred thousand pounds. Because the crawfish has generally a one-year life cycle, these fluctuations in catch may be expected in the future. When adverse conditions affect the population, the catch falls drastically and the population may take several years to reach normal levels.*[385]

Broom observed that "the average person in Louisiana has little knowledge of the vast and growing commercial opportunities offered by the lobster-like 'mud bug' which reproduces in Louisiana in astounding numbers."[386] He noted that the U.S. Soil Conservation Service at Crowley in Acadia Parish, LSU and the Louisiana Wildlife and Fisheries Commission were working to establish a crawfish research program.[387]

Funding for research came from a variety of state and federal sources that combined to form the Cooperative Wildlife and Fisheries Unit. The unit, which became the basis of LSU's aquaculture school, was made possible by cooperative agreements between LSU, the U.S. Fish and Wildlife Service and the Louisiana Wildlife and Fisheries Commission. As the knowledge base was gathered, local county agents and other officials with the LSU Agricultural Extension Service educated the public and, more importantly, future crawfish farmers of the new opportunities made possible by the prolific crawfish.[388]

One of the early print publications was the twelve-page *Grow Crawfish in Rice Fields* booklet issued by the Louisiana Agricultural Extension Service. Co-written in 1963 by Lewis Hill and E.A. Cancienne, the booklet speculated that the "Louisiana crawfish may well become a gourmet's delight throughout the North American continent, rivaling the Stone Crab of Cuba and the Maine lobster."[389]

Cancienne and Hill made their recommendations on field preparation, pond management and harvesting by using data gathered at the farms of Voorhies Trahan, Causby Hammic Jr. and Roland Faulk. The pamphlet included photos from the ponds.[390] *Grow Crawfish in Rice Fields* also plainly stated that there was room for plenty more research.[391]

Cecil LaCaze was one of the first students to come out of LSU's infant aquaculture program begun in 1963. His graduate thesis is "the first known thesis in Louisiana on the biology of red shrimp and white river crawfish."[392]

The *Sunday Advocate* reported that the university's Cooperative Fishery Unit, not yet called an aquaculture program, had eleven graduate students, "some of whom will likely continue work on the production of crawfish at LSU and its substations."[393] It was an exciting time for young researchers. The Louisiana crawfish field was wide open, and questions regarding bait, trap design, pond design and harvest efficiencies all needed answers.

In 1966, LaCaze was hired by the Louisiana Wildlife and Fisheries Commission,[394] while James W. Avault Jr., a native of East St. Louis, Illinois, was appointed to head up LSU's fledgling aquaculture program. Avault's PhD was from Auburn University, one of the leading aquaculture schools at the time.[395] He replaced a scholar who had started assembling an LSU program but left the university to take a job at Auburn. With Avault's hire, LSU took the lead role in crawfish aquaculture research.[396]

Avault said that when he was making the introductory rounds at Louisiana landowner and agricultural stakeholder meetings, his job description always drew a few laughs. "Professor Leslie Glasgow invited me to attend a hunting club supper which would celebrate the deer hunting season," Avault said. "I [told the group] that I was interested in doing crawfish farming research. That got a lot of laughs—someone in the audience hollered out, 'You don't have to farm them; in the spring you can pick them up along the highway.'"[397]

That was sometimes true, but the basin crop always depended on Mother Nature. Viosca had discovered that a dry summer was needed to encourage crawfish to burrow, control fish predators and aid a new growth of vegetation. A good crawfish year also needed a wet fall to flush the crawfish out of their holes and move the old water through the swamp. A mild winter allowed crawfish to grow.[398] When nature occasionally created these perfect conditions, everything was right with the world, according to Basin fishermen. But to think that they could be repeated year in and year out was asking a lot of the earth mother.

"The farmer, however, can control these factors," Avault said. "Our very first experiment conducted was in plastic-lined pools. We had no research

LSU Aquaculture researchers on a rear-wheel drive boat in St. Martin Parish. The boat is equipped with a front-end "seeder" used in research to "feed" crawfish in the 1980s. *Jim Avault/LSU AgCenter.*

ponds at that time. The crawfish grew very well on commercial fish feed, but the bottom line was not good. The feed cost as much as the crawfish could be sold for."[399]

Research cost money, too. Avault said the Sears and Roebuck aboveground pools he used to do the first experiments were necessary because the LSU farm out on Ben Hur Road had no crawfish ponds. Avault said aquaculture research may have been stuck in the mud if it weren't for the resourcefulness of Ubaldo E. Cossio, a Cuban farm worker. "He [Cossio] spoke virtually no English," Avault said. "Each morning, I would look for a stick and a place on the dirt to draw pictures for what he could do that day. Early on, he borrowed his brother-in-law's push lawnmower to mow what little land we had at Ben Hur Farm."[400]

Cossio conveyed to Avault that there was an unused World War II cable-operated bulldozer on the LSU farm that belonged to the USDA. Permission was granted for the aquaculture program to use the bulldozer. "However, we did not have money to buy diesel fuel," Avault said. "It was suggested then that Mr. Cossio get to know other farm managers at Ben Hur Farm. One such was man was sheep farm manager Mr. Reynolds. He gave us a fifty-five-gallon drum of diesel fuel. Mr. Cossio built our first pond."[401]

Anyone who takes a biology class learns that if a handful of straw is allowed to lie in a pan of water for some time, microscopic animals called paramecium will begin to proliferate. With that in mind, Avault began studying rice culture.[402]

During rice harvest, though the plant's stalk is cut and the grain separated by the harvesting machinery, the rice stubble continues to grow like grass on a lawn. A second crop, called a ratoon crop, could be grown if optimally managed. Most farmers don't worry about the stubble and won't return to the field until the following spring. With a wet fall, rice fields do what they are designed to do: hold water.

Voorhies Trahan and other rice farmers knew crawfish could coexist with the rice culture, and researchers proved rice fields could be seeded with crawfish if necessary.[403] What they didn't know was exactly how crawfish lived through the rice year and what they ate. Research determined that crawfish fed not on the decaying rice stubble but on the periphyton that accumulated in a wet autumn rice field.

"Among other things, you could say the crawfish is a detritivore—they feed on detritus and the associated organisms. And I guess you could say crawfish are omnivores. They'll eat anything," Avault said. "Jimmy Boyce said one of the best baits he had was dead snake."[404]

To researchers, the idea that a farmer could get two crops a year out of one piece of land was terrific. Not so fast, the rice farmers told Avault:

There was a big problem. At the time when we made this new technology available, the market for rice was quite good. The best, most profitable time to trap crawfish is March/April. That's when you plant rice. So the farmers are saying, "Look, I know this is a new technology, but I don't want to put money out for traps and I don't wanna fight with poachers. And in south Louisiana, we like to plant rice in March." And that's when you're right in the middle of harvesting crawfish. The point being the technology sat on the shelf for some years.[405]

A 1963 *Wall Street Journal* article discussed the connection between rice farming and crawfish and quoted John Ruppert of Crowley. The article speculated that crawfish farming in rice fields would become popular because Louisiana rice farmers were hampered by the U.S. government's "strict [rice] acreage controls."[406]

Writer Fred L. Zimmerman noted that southwest Louisiana rice farmers were going to produce more than $560,000 worth of "fish during the coming season" because crawfish tail meat was "showing up increasingly on Louisiana restaurant menus."[407] The article also mentioned upcoming scientific reports from LSU on the crawfish life cycle and the effects of rice pesticide on the crustacean.[408]

Ruppert, a rice/crawfish farmer, also dabbled in the tail-meat market. Supply was short even though he had 450 acres in crawfish production.[409]

Though the Atchafalaya Basin could not be depended on to bring in a steady crop every year, "deepwater" crawfish production grew, probably because more fishermen were entering the market. In 1960, the crawfish catch was 717,200 pounds. In 1969, a record high of 3 million pounds worth $500,000 dockside was brought to market.[410] These numbers include the farmed crawfish harvest that was barely seven thousand acres in 1968.[411]

If southwestern Louisiana rice farmers were showing restrained interest in raising crawfish, St. Martin Parish (where the crawfish industry was blooming) landowners and entrepreneurs wanted to know more about how crawfish pond management could maximize profits from the acres of marginal land that bordered the Atchafalaya Basin. In 1968, of the 7,000 total acres of state crawfish ponds, 5,060 were set in wooded ponds and rice fields in St. Martin Parish.[412]

The Louisiana Crawfish Industry Development Association (LCIDA) was formed in 1965 and included representation from the entire industry

A St. Martin Parish crawfish farmer walks his pond and lifts a "pillow" trap. Walking ponds is still common in 2013, but the pyramid trap is the current standard. *Courtesy* Teche News.

(the east and west side of the basin, crawfish farms, processors, brokers and restaurants),[413] but it soon became clear that there were divergent interests within the group. Headed by Representative J. Burton Angelle of Breaux Bridge, the group promoted crawfish research and wanted to "push a U.S. Corps of Engineers project to bring fresh water into the Atchafalaya Basin."[414]

Crawfish/rice farmer Roland Faulk said that the Basin crawfish trappers were sometimes overly insistent on what they wanted the corps to do about water levels:

> *I went to a crawfish meeting at Pat's Restaurant and there was a bunch of drunk fishermen in there, and they started raising hell with the Corps of Engineers. They had two people from the Corps of Engineers—a colonel and a captain—and they were trying to explain something about a dam or something further up. One guy stood up and said, "Well y'all haven't gotten off y'all's asses. We're gonna go blow 'em up tonight." They turned around and started to walk out the door, and they started a fight. They were gonna go blow that dam up. "We want more water, we want less water"—I don't know what they wanted, really.[415]*

The Atchafalaya River had been physically altered by man before, and now crawfish were economically altering the system. Crawfishermen were enjoying the increased profits from the burgeoning crawfish market and wanted to be able to rely on that market. The dockside value of the basin catch was $2,496 in 1950. In 1965, it was nearly $250,000, and it topped $600,000 in 1969. The catch value dropped to $329,011 in 1971 but skyrocketed to more than $1 million in 1974, the year after the Morganza Spillway was opened to avert a serious break in the Mississippi River levees.[416]

It was obvious to deepwater crawfishermen that the difference between a good year and a bad year was the mark on the flood stage gauge at Cairo, Illinois—forty feet at Cairo meant ten to fourteen feet of water in the basin.[417] However, the U.S. Corps of Engineers did not want to make a habit of altering the water flow of the Red, Atchafalaya and Mississippi Rivers just because a few crawfishermen wanted them to. The safe bet was to develop crawfish farming methods that could control water flow and predators and take advantage of the crawfish biological life cycle.

Jim Fowler was hired in 1970 by LSU to disseminate aquaculture information.[418] "They needed people to answer the questions that people had about catfish farming," Fowler said. "In the '70s, everybody thought catfish was going to be the thing, but crawfish came along and was put on the top shelf. The first interest was in the Breaux Bridge and Acadia area because they were already doing it."[419]

Fowler got busy right away and helped arrange the April 30, 1970 organizational meeting of the Louisiana Crawfish Farmers Association in Thibodaux.[420] Crawfish pond owner Clifford Hebert of Breaux Bridge was chosen as the first president.[421]

In 1971, Fowler and Cecil LaCaze (and, later, Larry de la Bretonne Jr.) became the preachers of crawfish, and their dissemination of agricultural research, called extension, provoked even more interest. The main piece of information was that well-managed ponds could produce one thousand pounds of crawfish per acre.

As Avault's graduate students completed their degree programs, many of them began to fill niches in the burgeoning crawfish research field. Robert Romaire began an outfield research program in 1980.[422] At the University of Louisiana at Lafayette, located in the heart of crawfish country, Don Gooch, Rusty Gaude and Jay Huner studied crawfish production efficiency.[423]

Scientists examined pond construction, monocropping and crop rotation systems, water quality, trapping methods, harvesting equipment, bait and baiting strategies, predation control, nuisance wildlife management and marketing and made recommendations on how to get the most crawfish out of the pond.[424]

Avault delivered a paper on Louisiana's crawfish farming system at an international symposium on crawfish in 1972. The main purpose of the conference was to discuss the demise of Europe's "noble crawfish"—*Astacus astucus*—which had fallen prey to disease. Louisiana's red swamp crawfish is immune to the disease, and there was some interest in importing the Cajun crustacean to Sweden for that country's annual *kräftskiva*. He suggested the group form the International Association of Astacology and invited the conference to Baton Rouge.[425]

In 1974, the international crawfish market was focused on Baton Rouge for the Second International Symposium on Freshwater Crayfish. Archduke Andreas Salvator Habsburg was among those who attended the conference. The Habsburgs ruled most of Europe all the way up until the twentieth century and are part of the reason *Astacus* was known as the "noble crawfish"—at one time, only nobles were allowed to eat crawfish. Reinhard Spitzy, the aide to Joachim von Ribbentrop of the Third Reich, and one Aubrey Heumann of Breaux Bridge also attended the symposium. Heumann was part owner of Mr. Crawfish, a St. Martin Parish crawfish-peeling plant.[426] Heumann inadvertently upset the Europeans when he served Breaux Bridge's signature dish, crawfish étouffée:

Farm-raised crawfish are harvested with "pyramid" traps. The catch is easily dumped into the boat's sorting bin and the trap re-baited through the opening at the top. *Burt Tietje.*

[The Europeans] *thought it was a terrible thing because over there, a crawfish feast is six individual crawfish per person. You eat them very slowly. You break off a claw, suck the juice, get the meat and you drink a glass of schnapps or aquavit. And then you do the other claw and drink another glass of schnapps or aquavit. It's a ritual. And so six is about all the crawfish that you can handle after all that drinking. So Aubrey made crawfish étouffée, and he reduced the noble crawfish* Astacus—*only it was Louisiana crawfish and not the noble crawfish—to a little piece of meat, and that was blasphemy.*[427]

Whatever faux pas Heumann may have committed was forgiven when Avault and his team treated the guests to a Louisiana crawfish boil. "We boiled one ton of crawfish for the visitors, and they were spread out all over tables set up in Parker Coliseum," Avault said. "They thought they had gone to heaven."[428]

Avault also arranged for the visitors to have their own version of Breaux Bridge's crawfish races, and representatives from each country were assigned a crawfish for the symposium's tournament. A filly crawfish Avault named Clovis (*klo-vees*) won the international race for the Swedes. The Breaux Bridge attendees immediately extended a challenge to Avault to enter Clovis in the Crawfish Festival's races, which was only two weeks away.

Heywood Hale Broun, a television broadcaster famous for calling the Kentucky Derby, was a special guest of the Crawfish Festival, and he called the crawfish races.[429] Broun described a scene of "dancing in the streets that brought [Peter] Bruegel's picture to life" and a race of "shelly steeds…under the weight of such names as Beaurgard, Aristotle and Alfonse [going] to the starting gates with little of the ceremony associated with larger derbies."[430]

It turned out that Clovis won the race going away:

Heywood Hale Broun was there, and he interviewed me. He said, "Well, Clovis has won the race at the International Crawfish Meeting, and now she's won here!" I said, "Yes, we've had her in training. We wanted to work with her because male crawfish often have big claws and don't move as fast. So she had relatively small claws. Further, we had a special diet for Clovis." Heywood Hale Broun said, "What do you feed her?" And I said, "Raw meat and gunpowder."[431]

By 1980, researchers had been working closely with crawfish farmers for more than twenty years and had learned a great deal about growing crawfish in woodlands near the Atchafalaya Basin and the rice fields of southwestern Louisiana. Double-cropping crawfish and rice was proving to be profitable, but farmers were doing fine producing rice alone. Even so, by 1982, crawfish pond acreage had grown from 7,000 in 1967 to 65,974 acres.[432] Then rice

Jeff Davis Parish crawfish farmer Burt Tietje runs traps in a boat designed to float on water or travel over levees. Twelve thousand traps can be checked and 1,500 pounds harvested daily in peak season with a boat like this. *Burt Tietje.*

commodity prices dropped through the cellar.[433] "Rice farmers were lucky to break even," Avault said. "Then they tried this crawfish rotation."[434]

In one year, acreage devoted to crawfish farming increased 53 percent and doubled in six years to 131,900 acres. Just over one thousand farmers were raising crawfish in 1982—in 1986, that number had risen to 1,835.[435]

The addition of 20 million pounds of crawfish to the supply caused a big ripple in the market, and prices suffered. The value of 1982's 49-million-pound catch was $35 million. In 1985, the 65-million-pound catch brought in only $31 million.[436] Prices continued to head south.[437]

The Breaux Bridge Crawfish Festival, with no other motive than to bring publicity to the town and make a few dollars in the meantime, had been the number-one marketing arm of the crawfish industry. The Louisiana Crawfish Farmers Association (LCFA) decided it had to expand the market. Everyone knew that most of Louisiana's crawfish was consumed in Louisiana, thus the market was competing for the same dollar. Naturally, prices would be soft. In 1984, the LCFA hosted its first trade show at Lafayette's Hilton Hotel to showcase the industry and its various products.[438]

After rice prices tanked in 1982, crawfish pond acreage doubled, and the industry held its first trade show in 1984 in Lafayette, Louisiana, prompting grown men to dress in crawfish costumes. *Jim Avault.*

The convention borrowed a few tricks from the Breaux Bridge Crawfish Festival, holding crawfish races, serving pounds and pounds of boiled crawfish and featuring cooking demonstrations. Crawfish aquaculture interests featured twenty booths demonstrating farming techniques. LCFA spokesperson Jane Barnett said the show "let restaurateurs and food buyers around the country know that crawfish farmers can supply the tasty crustaceans year round."[439]

Finally, the Cajun crustacean had the big-time marketing it deserved.

CRAWFISH STEW-FAY

This is a classic étouffée from south Louisiana. It's called a "stew-fay" simply because of the slurry (a combination of water and flour) that's added to thicken it up a bit.

¼ pound (1 stick) unsalted butter
2 cups chopped yellow onions
1 cup chopped green bell peppers
½ cup chopped celery
2 pounds peeled crawfish tails
1 tablespoon all-purpose flour dissolved in ½ cup water
Salt and cayenne

2 tablespoons chopped green onions
1 tablespoon chopped fresh parsley leaves
Cooked long-grain rice

Heat the butter over medium heat in a large, heavy pot. Add the onions, bell peppers and celery and cook, stirring until soft and lightly golden (eight to ten minutes). Add the crawfish and cook, stirring occasionally, until they begin to throw off a little liquid (about five minutes). Add the water/flour mixture, reduce the heat to medium-low and cook, stirring occasionally, until the mixture thickens (three to four minutes). Season with salt and cayenne. Remove from the heat. Add the green onions and parsley. Serve in bowls over rice.

—Rhena B. Bienvenu and Marcelle Bienvenu

CHAPTER 8

THAT PESKY SUPPLY-AND-DEMAND THING

Traditionally, crawfish farmers got higher prices because their controlled pond environments could bring in an early crop. The spring rise of the Atchafalaya Basin delivered a natural "deepwater" catch of larger crawfish because they had more time to mature. Demand rose for crawfish during the Lenten period because Louisiana's Catholic culture abstained from eating meat. The weeks leading up to Easter generally coincided with increased production and kept prices fairly steady, but come Easter Monday, with supply at its peak, demand began to drop. The week after Easter, crawfish buyers lowered the price across the board.[440] When Easter came early, crawfish producers grumbled very loudly because they knew the market would go to pot with a lot of fishing left to do. All of these economic principles were exacerbated in 1983 by the largest supply of crawfish Louisiana had ever seen.[441]

Prices were already low from the increase in pond production going into the spring. The 1983 basin catch was a decent 10 million pounds, and 1984's 12-million pound catch was even better.[442] But on April 26, dockside prices dropped sharply for Basin crawfish, and the fishermen called for a "fish-out."[443]

John Roe Sr. of Morgan City was the spokesman for the Basin crawfishermen. He was also the vice-president of the Louisiana Crawfish Producers Association, a group composed mostly of Basin crawfishermen. Roe claimed that the basin was having a bad year. Price-wise, the fishermen *were* having a bad year. An overnight ten-cent price drop the week after Easter, the end of the Catholic Lenten fast, was just too much for the swampers to take.[444] "The processors did the wrong thing in lowering the price to us just because it was the week after Easter," Roe said. "What really ticked us off is that they lowered our price but didn't pass it on to the consumers. We're tired of being kept poor by unscrupulous dealers, and we're going to continue this fish-out—we're not calling it a strike—until our price is raised to at least thirty-five cents per pound."[445]

For a weekend, the crawfishermen held steady. With the fervor of overworked coal miners, as many as nine hundred fishermen refused to fish. A May 2 Associated Press report from Henderson said the buyers had agreed to pay the thirty-five cents, but only for large crawfish.

Crawfisherman Sherbin Collette of Henderson attended a strike meeting in Pierre Part. "They were looking at me kinda funny because they knew some of us in Henderson were still fishing," Collette said. "We were still getting a higher price, but I had to show them my tickets. We decided not to fish for a few days, though.[446]

Eight days later, the crawfishermen claimed the dealers had broken their promise and called for a second strike. By the end of May, the crawfish season was essentially over. Al Scramuzza, a large New Orleans seafood retailer who sold as much as 150,000 pounds of crawfish a week, said the price went up but only because of the "natural shortage" associated with the end of the season. Scramuzza claimed when the weather gets hot, crawfish move to "cooler, deeper water, where they are more difficult to catch."[447]

Roe said the season was, in fact, near the end, but not because of the reasons Scramuzza cited. Roe said crabs move up into the lower Atchafalaya depending on water temperatures and enter crawfish traps. When crabs move into crawfish traps, they eat the crawfish, and that is usually a signal to the fishermen to pick up their traps.[448]

Roe claimed the victory for the east Basin crawfishermen. "This is the first time fishermen in the Basin have banded together for a cause, and this is the first successful strike in the fishing industry in the Atchafalaya Basin," Roe said."[449] Membership in the LCPA, which had been formed in 1983 in the living room of a Pierre Part fisherman,[450] increased from two hundred to six hundred.

"We do feel, though, that on the whole, the strike was tremendously successful," Roe said. "We had 100 percent positive feedback, and [the dealers] were no longer dealing with individual fishermen but rather with a viable and powerful force."[451]

The supply had grown. Obviously, the market needed to grow, and for any endeavor to grow, it needs money. The industry began by assessing a fee on the sale of artificial baits. The money funded the Louisiana Crawfish Promotion and Research Board in 1983, and marketing efforts were begun.[452]

Other peculiar factors helped to extend the market share of crawfish and Cajunism. The oil bust of the 1980s created a second *Grand Dérangement*. Cajuns and other Louisiana workers were basically expelled again from their homeland to find work in Atlanta, Dallas and Houston. But just because they had to leave Louisiana didn't mean they had to do without crawfish, dark-roast coffee and Mardi Gras king cakes. The migration created a secondary shipping market of Cajun delicacies to far-flung locations.

Bill Pizzolato of Tony's Seafood in Baton Rouge, one of the current premier seafood dealers of Louisiana, sent Cajun care packages all over the country. "There used to be big planes that would fly out of Baton Rouge on a Thursday," Pizzolato said. "We'd load them down with fifteen thousand pounds of seafood. We got into shipping because people wanted us to ship them live crawfish and boiled crawfish, and now it's just part of the business. That was all new."[453]

The Louisiana Department of Agriculture and Forestry (LDAF), under Commissioner Bob Odom, began an international and national marketing program to educate the world about Cajun food products, including crawfish. Numerous media events put together by the LDAF featured Cajun cooking demonstrations by Chef Paul "K-Paul" Prudhomme in Oregon, London and New York City. Prudhomme "won" a number of "Crawfish Culinary Cook-Offs" against Oregon chef Marcel Lahsene, and West Coast media recorded it all. National news anchorman Dan Rather reported the story of the cook-off and the growing crawfish industry in the June 28, 1985 broadcast of the *CBS Evening News*.[454]

The marketing and media attention paid off, and national restaurant chains began having conversations with Louisiana crawfish stakeholders. Interest in crawfish by the national restaurant trade came as early as 1980, when the Bennigan's Restaurant chain held a large crawfish boil for a St. Patrick's Day celebration in the parking lot of its new Cortana Mall restaurant in Baton Rouge. The LSU Cooperative Extension Service arranged for a Crawfish Technology and Marketing Conference and invited more than two hundred crawfish processors to attend the seminar. Representatives of Bennigan's and Red Lobster told the group how to break into the national market.[455]

"How many of you have 5,000 pounds of fresh crawfish meat in your freezers?" asked Kress Muenzmay of Red Lobster. No one responded.

"That's not an underutilized product," he said. Muenzmay cautioned the crawfish stakeholders "to take their time developing the market and avoid trying to make a killing by exploiting surges in the market."[456]

Bennigan's did order crawfish—a lot of crawfish. Odom said the 178-restaurant chain wanted "20,000 pounds of frozen crawfish tails every day of the season, which runs from early fall to midsummer."[457] Bennigan's would serve a fried crawfish product they dubbed "Cajun Popcorn." They also wanted to serve étouffée and a crawfish jambalaya.

Odom built a twenty-four-thousand-square-foot freezer in St. Martinville for nineteen Louisiana processors contracted by Bennigan's to provide the restaurant with the 700,000 pounds of tail meat. The purpose of the facility was to wash the crawfish fat from the meat and repackage it according to Bennigan's standards.[458] He envisioned a warehouse cold-storage facility that would be the crawfish's gateway to the national market.[459]

Everyone in the industry was optimistic. The market, which had just doubled, could continue to increase. Americans coast to coast would love crawfish once they tasted the Cajun crustacean. Many experts thought northeastern Louisiana farmers would begin installing crawfish ponds and that processing plants would be established north of Alexandria.

Jane Barnett, the spokesperson for the Louisiana Crawfish Farmers Association, predicted that if the crawfish industry could make good on the contract and provide a quality product, "the number of acres in pond production will increase dramatically as a result."[460]

LSU Agriculture Extension agent Larry de la Bretonne believed Louisiana crawfish pond acreage would top 250,000 acres by 1990.[461] "Crawfish is one of the best crops a farmer can integrate into his ongoing agricultural interests," de la Bretonne said. "The farmer has the equipment and the land, and he has the labor that's mostly idle during the winter months. With the serious problems we're facing in so many of our other major crops, I see more and more people getting into crawfish production."[462]

Sadly, the Louisiana crawfish market was still immature and made all the mistakes that Muenzmay warned them against.

LDAF international marketing director Roy Johnson said the processing plant had trouble fulfilling its quota. "If prices went up, some of the processors sold their meat to other customers."[463] Bennigan's stopped buying, and no other national restaurant chain stepped forward.

The setback didn't stop crawfish marketing efforts, though. Going back to square one, the Louisiana Crawfish Promotion and Research Board funded a market survey in 1990.[464] It must have been astonished by the report. Barbara Miller of Venture Associates in Baton Rouge told the board that short-term, limited market increases could be attained with a "modest increase in funding." Modest, according to Venture Associates, was $1.3 to $3.3 million.[465] "By most industry standards, it takes about $10 million in advertising to 'cut through the clutter' of competing products," Miller said.[466] The LDAF press release announcing the report results flatly stated that "that level of funding is not available."[467]

The report, however, advised dropping the word "mudbug" in crawfish marketing.[468] Renaming a delicacy is easily done. You just stop using the word in your press releases. In other words, talk is cheap. "If we are going to sell crawfish, it has to have a clean image—pristine clean—to overcome the mudbug connotation," she said.[469]

Undeterred, the Cajun crustacean made its way to Swedish and French tables as a result of the LDAF's international marketing efforts. Johnson made several trips to Europe to learn about the continental crawfish market.[470]

After Baton Rouge hosted the Second International Symposium on Freshwater Crayfish in 1974, Louisiana producers hoped they could supply the Swedish market. The Swedes chose the Turkish crawfish instead. However, the Turkish crawfish fell to the same disease that killed the noble crawfish, and the Swedes found themselves shopping around for a crawfish again in 1988.

"The red swamp crawfish is immune to the disease," Johnson said. "But the Swedes wanted the biggest crawfish, so if we were going to sell them crawfish, we had to learn to grade them. That's where the now-common practice of grading began."[471]

Johnson said the Swedish market was rather small, about 8 million pounds, but Louisiana grabbed a share. Swedish representatives came to the Bayou State and taught Klein Seafood of Baton Rouge and Louisiana Crawfish Wholesalers of St. Martinville how to cook crawfish Swedish-style.[472]

Johnson said a clever marketing campaign harkening back to catch phrases of the Cold War teased the Scandinavian people with a billboard featuring a picture of a red crawfish next to the phrase, "The Reds from the West Are Coming."[473]

The reviews of the Louisiana crawfish served Swedish-style were very favorable. Odom said the chef and food writer critiques were just as important to a crawfish producer as a New York critic's review of a Broadway show.[474] Fortunately, the notices were good, and Louisiana crawfish producers enjoyed the Swedish market for five years.

Why only five years?

Workers grade crawfish with an early version of a crawfish-sorting machine. *Jim Avault/ LSU AgCenter.*

"The Swedes are sharp businessmen, and it didn't take them long to find Chinese crawfish," Johnson said.[475]

Cajun proponent Revon Reed said the crawfish is the only animal that will not leave its post when faced with the onslaught of a coming train.[476] The Cajun crustacean, however, had never seen a locomotive like the Reds from the East.

For several years, Chinese crawfish lurked around the edges of the market. Restaurants and other retail outlets were using them but kept it relatively hush-hush. A 1996 *Advocate* article revealed that many of the food vendors at the esteemed New Orleans Jazz & Heritage Festival were using Chinese crawfish.[477] It was an embarrassing debut, kind of like a drunk uncle at Christmas.

"The Chinese have taken over the crawfish pies, étouffée, file gumbo and most other crawfish dishes at the huge outdoor festival," wrote *Advocate* reporter Mary Foster. "The crawfish from overseas are too cheap to pass up."[478]

How did Chinese crawfish get to Louisiana? First, a Louisiana bullfrog brought them to Japan from New Orleans, and later, Louisiana merchants invited them back.

It seems almost too incredible to believe, but the Chinese crawfish is the long-lost cousin of the Cajun crustacean.

Cecil LaCaze, an early crawfish researcher, wrote in the May–June 1966 *Louisiana Conservationist* that the Japanese imported Louisiana bullfrogs in 1918. To feed the bullfrogs, the Japanese brought in Louisiana's red swamp crawfish in 1930.[479] The crawfish were supplied by Percy Viosca Jr.[480]

By 1951, Matsuzo Ueno, director of the Otsu Hydrobiological Station at Otsu-shi, Shigaken, said the red swamp crawfish had become a pest, causing serious damage to the rice crop.[481]

Years later, in the mid-1980s, Tetsuya Suko of Saitama University in Urawa, Japan, visited LSU's aquaculture school and read a paper titled *Status of Crawfish in Japan*. Suko's paper, which reiterated LaCaze's 1966 information, stated that "about 100 individuals were brought to Japan from New Orleans in 1932." Of the 100, only 20 crawfish survived the transpacific trip.[482] The crawfish were released into the frog culture ponds. The bullfrogs loved the crawfish, but the crawfish ate the bullfrogs, too. A rainstorm and subsequent flooding collapsed the culture pond, and the crawfish escaped.[483]

Crawfish were brought to China in the 1930s by the Japanese. The people of the Jiangsu area believed the Japanese military was trying to destroy the Chinese rice crop by unleashing *Procambrus clarkii*. Fifty years later, crawfish had become a major food product available for export and a delicacy in Nanjing, where it was "becoming too luxurious" to eat in restaurants. The favored recipe of the area is called "Nanjing little lobster."[484]

But how did the Chinese crawfish get to Louisiana? Well, Louisiana businessmen invited the Chinese crawfish.

In 1988, the governor of the Chinese province of Guizhou met twice with Louisiana crawfish businessmen and Ag Commissioner Bob Odom to discuss the exportation of crawfish technology and equipment to China.[485] According to the LDAF press release, the technology included pond construction, growing, harvesting and processing. The Chinese delegation had also invested $500,000 to set up an office and hire salespeople to establish a Louisiana-based import-export business.[486] Guizhou's major crops were rice and sugarcane (just like Louisiana); its climate was hot and humid (just like Louisiana); and farmers could grow crawfish there (just like Louisiana). The capitalist Louisiana crawfish industry didn't have money to market its crawfish, but the Chinese socialist government did.[487]

Elton Bernard of Cottonport formed Bernard Seafood Company and began shipping crawfish from China to Louisiana because "top-grade Louisiana crawfish was expensive and hard to get."[488] Bernard, of

Cajun heritage, arranged for idle Chinese shrimp-processing plants to peel crawfish and gave Chinese workers at twenty-seven processing plants housing and the equivalent of nine dollars for a sixty-hour workweek.[489] He quickly became known as the "King of Chinese Crawfish."[490]

At first, "people laughed" at the Chinese product. "Crawfish is to Louisiana what wine is to France," wrote Donna St. George of the *New York Times* in 1991.[491] The product didn't make too much of a market splash because Louisiana production was good—more than 107 million pounds in 1989 and 119 million in 1989. But three lean seasons followed.[492] Prices for Louisiana tail meat rose sharply, and merchants who were capitalizing on Cajunism more than ever went with the Chinese crawfish.[493]

Using Chinese crawfish in Cajun recipes didn't seem to bother restaurateurs. Other non-Cajun manufacturers had been exploiting Cajunism for years. A north Louisiana company marketed Cajun Cola. An Arizona condiment company produced something they called Kickin' Cajun Hot Sauce. Marvel Comics introduced a Cajun character named Gambit. There were even "Cajun" pictorials in adult magazines.[494] If the public was willing to accept supposed Cajun products from non-Cajun sources, certainly they could accept Chinese crawfish in Cajun recipes.

Food vendor Clark Hoffpauer, who specialized in serving the Cajun culture's signature crawfish étouffée recipe at the 1996 New Orleans Jazz & Heritage Festival, alleged the festival was about the heritage, not economics, but he abandoned the Cajun crustacean for the cheaper Chinese meat: "I had to go to the Chinese tails. They're at least $2 a pound cheaper, and when you talk 1,700 pounds, that's quite of bit of change. I'd rather use Louisiana crawfish. After all, this is about Louisiana heritage, but business is business."[495]

Retailers could sell tail meat that had been caught, processed and frozen in China and shipped more than eight thousand miles for $3.99 a pound. The homegrown product was $7.99.[496]

In 1992, Odom began to try to put the genie back in the bottle. He seized twelve tons of Chinese crawfish tail meat at the New Orleans Cold Storage Warehouse because the packages were improperly labeled by weight. The labels showed the packages weighed one pound but didn't have the net weight printed on the bag.[497] Naturally, lawsuits ensued.

The U.S. importers were tricky. They labeled their crawfish product with Cajun-sounding names like "Bernard's Real Cajun Brand" and "Boudreaux's Crawfish" and put "Product of China" somewhere on the label in smaller print.[498]

Odom used every weapon in his arsenal. He had the crawfish tested for cholera. None was found.[499] He had them tested for banned antibiotics. Banned substances were found, but the logistics of testing every Chinese shipment of crawfish (and fighting every lawsuit) were unmanageable.[500]

Finally, the International Trade Commission determined that the Chinese had dumped their product on the United States market in 1997, and a tariff was ordered. The importers tried to circumvent the ruling and relabeled the crawfish as a "Product of Singapore." Odom dispatched Roy Johnson to the island state and found there was no crawfish production in Singapore. Odom seized fourteen thousand pounds of the sham Singapore product. More lawsuits followed.[501]

In 1992, Representative Dirk DeVille of Ville Platte introduced a bill requiring restaurants to indicate on their menus if they served "imported" crawfish.[502] The measure was successfully opposed by the Louisiana Restaurant Association until Representative Fred Mills of Breaux Bridge got the "Ask Before You Eat" law passed in 2008.[503]

But by then, it was almost too late. Of the 102 processors that were in business before Chinese crawfish hit, fewer than 12 of them were still operating in 2004.

The Louisiana crawfish will have a tough time competing with its Chinese cousin. Louisiana can produce about 100 million pounds of crawfish, but China is producing 1 billion.[504] In total, 90 percent of the Louisiana domestic tail-meat market has been lost to the Chinese.

Dwight Landreneau, an LSU AgCenter aquaculture marketing specialist, said the Chinese crawfish "strike at our culture, our food and our jobs. The crawfish industry is not major corporations. It's individual families."[505]

Since the tariff, a few processors have gotten back into the game. Adam Johnson of BayouLand Seafood in Henderson says there are now about twenty plants in operation.[506] Producers have also created increased demand for the Louisiana crawfish in the live market.[507] That's a lot of crawfish boils.

It's a safe bet to assume the peeled crawfish tails served in Louisiana's touristy restaurants are Chinese, and that's too bad. "The sad part is that a lot of people don't know the difference because they've never tasted crawfish," Chef Prudhomme said.[508] Leah Chase of New Orleans's Dooky Chase said, "The Chinese crawfish, in taste, is not bad. But nothing is better than a fresh thing. I like Louisiana crawfish because it's always fresher."[509]

But markets evolve. In 2011, Alain Schmit of Crawfresh Import SA in Luxembourg said Chinese tastes are changing. "Frozen tails are now being sold in supermarkets in Beijing," he said. "If this is successful, then they will be sold in supermarkets all round China and there will be very little left for export."[510]

Today, crawfish boiling rigs are common in Louisiana and can be located in a supermarket parking lot or a business for crawfish "to-go" or catered crawfish boils. *Sam Irwin.*

If you want to experience the real crawfish taste that made Breaux Bridge, Henderson and Lafayette famous, ask your server if that restaurant's crawfish were raised in Louisiana. They're supposed to tell you—it's the law. Better yet, visit Acadiana and seek out the restaurants and markets that serve fresh crawfish tail meat. My definition of fresh is meat that has never been frozen.

There's a little Cajun restaurant called D.I.'s on Evangeline Highway north of Jennings that is located pretty much in the middle of a crawfish pond. With a bit of *petit peut-être* (puh-teet, puh tet)—literally a little bit of maybe—owner D.I. Frugé started his own crawfish restaurant so far off the beaten path that you just about need a GPS to find it.[511] Like Pat Huval before him, Frugé traps his own crawfish. Pat fished in the Atchafalaya Basin, and D.I. fishes in his own pond—two different styles of crawfishing but the same Cajun crawfish.

Assuming you visit Louisiana because you want to try crawfish, insist on Louisiana crawfish. If you wanted to eat Chinese crawfish, I guess you'd vacation in China.

NOTES

CHAPTER 1

1. Malcolm Comeaux, *Atchafalaya Swamp Life: Settlement and Folk Occupations*, vol. 11 (Baton Rouge: Louisiana State University, School of Geosciences, 1972).
2. Carleton F. Pool, "Vast Commercial Possibilities of the Humble Louisiana Crawfish," *Times-Picayune*, February 4, 1923.
3. "Brief History of Creole Cooking in New Orleans, " Louisiana Digital Library, http://cdm16313.contentdm.oclc.org/cdm/compoundobject/collection/LWP/id/7629/rec/15.
4. Pool, "Vast Commercial Possibilities of the Humble Louisiana Crawfish."
5. Ibid.
6. Jay Huner, "World Crawfish Productions Numbers," e-mail message to author, September 26, 2013.
7. Wm. McG. Keefe, "Viewing the News," *Times-Picayune*, August 30, 1931.
8. Herman Joseph Jacobi, *The Catholic Family in Rural Louisiana* (Washington, D.C.: Catholic University of America, 1937).
9. Ibid.
10. Comeaux, *Atchafalaya Swamp Life*.
11. Huner, "World Crawfish Productions Numbers."
12. James H. Dormon, *People Called Cajuns: An Introduction to an Ethnohistory* (Lafayette: Center for Louisiana Studies, 1983).
13. Ibid.
14. Greg Guirard and C. Ray Brassieur, *Inherit the Atchafalaya* (Lafayette: Center for Louisiana Studies, 2007).
15. Jon L. Gibson, ed., *Archeology and Ethnology on the Edges of the Atchafalaya Basin, South Central Louisiana* (New Orleans: U.S. Army Corps of Engineers, 1982).
16. Guirard and Brassieur, *Inherit the Atchafalaya*.

17. Jay Huner and Mark Konikoff, "Wild-Caught Crawfish Management Plan Working Draft for Review and Comment." (Boyce, LA, May 2009).

18. Guirard and Brassieur, *Inherit the Atchafalaya*.

19. Harold Schoeffler, Interview, July 20, 2013.

20. Gibson, *Archeology and Ethnology*.

21. Antoinette DeBosier, "Easter Weekend on the West Guide Levee of the Atchafalaya," *Atchafalay Basin Program*, http://dnr.louisiana.gov/index.cfm?md=pagebuilder&tmp=home&pid=495.

22. Guirard and Brassieur, *Inherit the Atchafalaya*.

23. Marjorie R. Esman, *The Town That Crawfish Built* (Baton Rouge, LA: VAAPR Inc., 1984).

24. Ibid.

25. Ibid.

26. Dale Curry, "Good Food Puts Town on Map," *States-Item*, May 8, 1986.

27. Mary White, "Crawfish Tales," e-mail message to author, July 15, 2013.

28. Mable Enard Julian, Interview, August 28, 2013.

29. Gus Cranow, "Shunpiking: Off the Beaten Path," *Morning Advocate*, September 29, 1978.

30. Agnes Huval, Interview, October 2, 2013.

31. Esman, *The Town That Crawfish Built*.

32. Glen Pitre, *The Crawfish Book* (Jackson: University Press of Mississippi, 1993).

33. *Teche News*, "Commercial Processing First Began in 1949," April 22, 1982, Teche News Crawfish Supplement edition.

34. *Lafayette Telephone Directory*, 1959.

35. Sandy Plakidas, Interview, July 26, 2013.

36. *Breaux Bridge, Arnaudville, Cecilia, Henderson, Parks Telephone Directory*, 1984.

37. Terry Guidry, Interview, November 14, 2013.

38. Dormon, *People Called Cajuns*.

39. Ibid.

40. Floyd Knott, "Book (5:17 a.m.)," e-mail message to author, July 23, 2013.

41. Jacobi, *The Catholic Family*.

42. Plakidas, Interview.

43. James W. Avault Jr., Interview, July 23, 2013.

44. Jack Dale Delhomme, Interview, April 4, 2013.

45. Ibid.

CHAPTER 2

46. *Times-Picayune*, "Crawfish Cause Levee Trouble," June 7, 1908.

47. *St. Tammany Farmer*, "Death to the Crawfish," January 23, 1904.

48. Revon Reed, *Lâche Pas La Patate: Portrait Des Acadiens de La Louisiana* (Montreal: Editions Parti pris, 1976).

49. Jim Bradshaw, "Arrow Points and Place Names Are Reminders of Attakapas," *Daily Advertiser*, August 26, 1997.

50. Pitre, *The Crawfish Book*.

51. Malcolm Comeaux, "Historical Development of the Crayfish Industry in the United States" (presented at the Second International Symposium on Freshwater Crayfish) (Baton Rouge: Louisiana State University Division of Continuing Education, 1975), 609–20.

52. *Dictionary.com*, "Bisque," http://dictionary.reference.com/browse/bisque.

53. Po Tidholm, "The Crayfish Party," *The Official Gateway to Sweden*, http://web.archive.org/web/20090204020249/http://www.sweden.se/templates/cs/CommonPage____11371.aspx.

54. Renee Peck, "The Flavors of Finland," *Times-Picayune*, August 12, 1982.

55. Comeaux, "Historical Development of the Crayfish Industry."

56. Barry Jean Ancelet, *Cajun Country* (Jackson: University Press of Mississippi, 1991).

57. C. Paige Gutierrez, *Cajun Foodways* (Jackson: University Press of Mississippi, 1992).

58. Jerry G. Walls, *Crawfishes of Louisiana* (Baton Rouge: Louisiana State University Press, 2009).

59. Pool, "Vast Commercial Possibilities of the Humble Louisiana Crawfish."

60. *Weekly Thibodaux Sentinel*, "Local Paragraphs," April 27, 1901.

61. *Weekly Messenger*, "Local News," March 31, 1900.

62. Ibid., "Crawfish and Other Seafood," April 14, 1906.

63. Ibid., "Town Council," January 12, 1918.

64. Ibid., "If You Know a Business, Study Its Chances Here," May 22, 1915.

65. *Donaldsonville Chief*, "River Shrimp and Crawfish," June 25, 1921.

66. *St. Landry Clarion*, "Big Blow-Out at the K. of C. Hall," March 22, 1919.

67. Knott, "Book."

68. *Lafayette Advertiser*, "Carencro Budget," May 4, 1904.

69. Dean Tevis, "Tasty Crawfish Dishes Add to Teche Culinary Fame," *Beaumont Enterprise*, March 17, 1935.

70. Ibid.

71. Podine Schoenberger, "Fearless Little Crawfish Supplies Wayside Industry and Affords Family Sport," *Times-Picayune*, March 20, 1932.

72. Jacobi, *The Catholic Family*.

73. Ibid.

74. Huner and Konikoff, "Wild-Caught Crawfish Management Plan Working Draft for Review and Comment."

75. Ibid.

76. *State-Times*, "'Right to Work' Bill Is Passed by House; Referendum Is Killed," June 10, 1946.

77. Knott, "Book."

78. Mrs. K.C. Saxon, ed., "Society: Elks Supper Will Be Quite an Event," *Morning Advocate*, April 6, 1915.

79. Dickie Breaux, Interview, July 26, 2013.

80. LSU AgCenter, "2012 LSU AgCenter Agricultural Summary," http://www.lsuagcenter.com/agsummary/archive/2012/-State-Totals/2012StateTotals.pdf.

81. Ibid.

CHAPTER 3

82. James F. Hudson and Wildon J. Fontenot, *Profitability of Crawfish Peeling Plants in Louisiana* (Baton Rouge: LSU Agriculture Center, 1970).

83. James Nelson Gowanloch, "Crayfish in Louisiana," *Louisiana Conservationist*, 1951.

84. Ibid.

85. Jacobi, *The Catholic Family*.

86. Huner and Konikoff, "Wild-Caught Crawfish Management Plan Working Draft for Review and Comment."

87. Tevis, "Tasty Crawfish Dishes Add to Teche Culinary Fame."

88. "Commercial Processing First Began in 1949."

89. Esman, *The Town That Crawfish Built*.

90. Raymond Castille, "Raymond Castille Written Account of 1959 Breaux Bridge Centennial Celebration" (Raymond Castille, 1959).

91. J.S. Badon, "J.S. Badon News of Breaux Bridge," *Teche News*, April 7, 1960.

92. Pie Dufour, "Pie Dufour's à La Mode: Crayfish Center Set for Festival," *Times-Picayune*, March 29, 1959.

93. *Teche News*, "Breaux Bridge Centennial Planned for Celebration in March of 1958," November 27, 1958.

94. Knott, "Book."

95. *State-Times*, "S.I.A.A. Meet at Lafayette," May 12, 1928.

96. Nita Sims Breazeale, "Unique Places to Eat Are Found Up the Rivers and Down Bayous of Louisiana," *Morning Advocate*, May 14, 1935.

97. Tevis, "Tasty Crawfish Dishes Add to Teche Culinary Fame."

98. L.L. Bienvenu, "Statue of Evangeline to Be Unveiled Today at St. Martinville, La.," *Beaumont Enterprise*, April 19, 1931.

99. Ibid.

100. *State-Times*, "Tribute Is Paid Beauty of State by Party of Visiting Librarians," May 3, 1932.

101. A.J. Liebling, *The Earl of Louisiana* (Baton Rouge: Louisiana State University Press, 1970).

102. Pie Dufour, "Pie Dufour's à La Mode: Mudbugs Are Out in Force," *Times-Picayune*, April 3, 1955.

103. Mrs. Max Schenker, "Parish Library Pantry," *State-Times*, April 4, 1957.

104. Howard Jacobs, "Remoulade: 'Lovely Louisiana' Is Topflight Travel Guide," *Times-Picayune*, January 8, 1959.

105. Pat Huval, Interview, April 4, 2013.

106. Bob Scearce, "Set the Hook Hard," *Morning Advocate*, April 16, 1957.

107. Breaux, Interview.

108. Dufour, "Pie Dufour's à La Mode: Crayfish Center Set for Festival."

109. Breazeale, "Unique Places to Eat Are Found Up the Rivers and Down Bayous of Louisiana."

110. Tevis, "Tasty Crawfish Dishes Add to Teche Culinary Fame."

111. Johnny Raymond, Interview, August 1, 2013.

112. Mary Tutwiler, "Crawfish Tales," *Independent*, June 1, 2005.

113. Myra Miers, "Old Rendez-Vous Club Birthplace of Étouffée?" *Teche News*, 1978 Crawfish Festival supplement edition.

114. Ibid.

115. Tutwiler, "Crawfish Tales."

116. Miers, "Old Rendez-Vous Club Birthplace of Étouffée?"

117. Crawfish Festival Association, "Creation of Crawfish Étouffée" (Crawfish Festival Association, 1964).

118. Miers, "Old Rendez-Vous Club Birthplace of Étouffée?"

119. Breaux, Interview.

120. *Teche News*, "Breaux Bridge Centennial Planned for Celebration in March of 1958."

121. Ibid., "Centennial Belles Photo Cutline," April 2, 1959.

122. *Times-Picayune*, "Breaux Bridge Group Sets Visit," March 25, 1959.

123. *Daily Advertiser*, "Kangaroo Court Fines Many of the Beardless," March 9, 1959.

124. Ibid., "Breaux Bridge Makes Plans to Celebrate Centennial," November 28, 1958.

125. Dufour, "Pie Dufour's à La Mode: Crayfish Center Set for Festival."

126. Ibid., "Pie Dufour's à La Mode: Mudbugs Are Out in Force."

127. Walls, *Crawfishes of Louisiana*.

128. Dale Irvin, Interview, July 15, 2013.

129. Zach Johnk, "Crawfish vs. Crayfish," e-mail message to author, August 13, 2013.

130. *Times-Picayune*, "Breaux Bridge Delegates Urge Beard for Governor," March 10, 1959.

131. Robert Wagner, "Hayes Says Gov. Long Is Bluffing About Running," *Times-Picayune*, April 13, 1959.

132. Margaret Dixon, "Governor Hayes Put Election on Long and Anti-Long Basis," *Morning Advocate*, April 13, 1959.

133. Ibid.

134. Michael L. Kurtz and Morgan D. Peoples, *Earl K. Long: The Saga of Uncle Earl and Louisiana Politics* (Baton Rouge: Louisiana State University Press, 1990).

135. Liebling, *The Earl of Louisiana*.

136. Walt Benton, "Around the Capitol," *Teche News*, April 23, 1959.

137. Kurtz and Peoples, *Earl K. Long*.

138. Jim LaCaffinie, "Thousands Join in Revelry as Breaux Bridge Starts Anniversary Celebration," *Morning Advocate*, April 11, 1959.

139. Ibid.

140. Claire Puneky, "Breaux Bridge Gets Ike Wire," *Times-Picayune*, April 12, 1959.

141. *Teche News*, "Centennial Events Plans by Breaux Bridge Negroes," April 2, 1959.

142. Breaux Bridge Centennial Committee, "Breaux Bridge Centennial Celebration Souvenir Program" (Centennial News, 1959).

143. Mack Johnson, "Hayes Charges Long 'Mocks' Constitution," *Daily Advertiser*, April 13, 1959.

144. Wagner, "Hayes Says Gov. Long Is Bluffing About Running."

145. Ibid.

146. Ibid.

147. Ed Clinton, "Politicians Get in a Word at Breaux Bridge Centennial," *State-Times*, April 13, 1959.

148. Wagner, "Hayes Says Gov. Long Is Bluffing About Running."

149. Pete Baird, "Picayunes," *Times-Picayune*, April 14, 1959.

150. Kurtz and Peoples, *Earl K. Long*.

151. Raymond Castille and Maxine Castille, Interview, January 18, 2013.

152. Ibid.

153. Jim LaCaffinie, "75,000 Jam Breaux Bridge to Celebrate Town's Centennial," *Morning Advocate*, April 13, 1959.

154. *Teche News*, "Three Days Celebration Is One of Biggest Events Ever Staged in St. Martin Parish," April 16, 1959.

155. LaCaffinie, "75,000 Jam Breaux Bridge to Celebrate Town's Centennial."

156. *Times-Picayune*, "Breaux Bridge Affair Is Attended by 20,000," April 13, 1959.

157. Ibid.

158. Charlene Harrison, "'There Wasn't One Arrest Made!'" *Teche News*, 1989, Crawfish edition.

159. Blackie Bienvenu, "This and That," *Teche News*, April 16, 1959.

160. LaCaffinie, "75,000 Jam Breaux Bridge to Celebrate Town's Centennial."

CHAPTER 4

161. Plakidas, Interview.

162. Carl Simon, Interview, January 10, 2013.

163. *Morning Advocate*, "Breaux Bridge Lions to Send Delegates to State Convention Here," March 6, 1957.

164. *Teche News*, "Eternal King Is Active Crawfish Ambassador," 1978 Crawfish Festival edition.

165. Harris Pellerin, Interview, July 13, 2013.

166. Delhomme, Interview.

167. Ibid.

168. Ibid.

169. Mikko Macchione and Kerri McCaffety, *Napoleon House* (New Orleans: Pelican Publishing Company, 2011).

170. Dianne Domingues, Interview, August 14, 2013.

171. Howard Jacobs, "Mudbug Sultan Gets Crawfish Coiffure," *Times-Picayune*, April 7, 1960.

172. Reed, *Lache Pas La Patate*.

173. Pellerin, Interview.

174. Blackie Bienvenu, "This and That," *Teche News*, April 30, 1960.

175. *Morning Advocate*, "Unveil Mural," September 15, 1961.

176. Gene Mearns, Interview, January 11, 2013.

177. Ken Grissom, Interview, September 11, 2013.

178. *Morning Advocate*, "Crawfish Plaques Given Queens," June 20, 1961.

179. Bob Rogers, "USL Student Crowned Sugar Industry Queen," *Morning Advocate*, September 30, 1962.

180. *Morning Advocate*, "Crawfish Plaque to Be Given Head of Jaycees," May 18, 1963.

181. Brenda Broussard, Interview, November 5, 2013.

182. *Morning Advocate*, "Eternal King Crawfish," February 25, 1965.

183. John Boss, "Awards First Colonel's Commission," *Morning Advocate*, May 17, 1972.

184. *Morning Advocate*, "Receives First License," October 31, 1965.

185. Ibid., "'C' Stands for Crawfish," January 6, 1968.

186. George Fawcett, "Kingfish Junior and King Crawfish," *Morning Advocate*, November 11, 1967.

187. *State-Times*, "Crawfish Season Opens, Festival Set April 15–17," April 11, 1966.

188. *Morning Advocate*, "King Proclaims Crawfish Time in Louisiana," January 24, 1968.

189. *Teche News*, "Eternal King Is Active Crawfish Ambassador."

190. Delhomme, Interview.

191. Carl Simon, Interview.

192. Pellerin, Interview.

193. Breaux, Interview.

194. Richard Collin and Rima Collin, *The New Orleans Cookbook* (New York: Alfred A. Knopf, 1975).

CHAPTER 5

195. *New York Times*, "Crawfish Blacken Road," August 8, 1933.

196. Ibid.

197. *Beaumont Enterprise*, "Pajamas Too Formal for Louisiana Governor Who Receives Uniformed High Army Officers in Underwear," June 5, 1930.

198. *Oxnard Press-Courier*, "Gourmet's Day On Highways," August 2, 1952.

199. Ibid.

200. James A. Daigle, "Crazy for Crawfish Story," e-mail message to author, July 28, 2013.

201. NOAA, "National Marine Fisheries Annual Commercial Landings Statistics," September 19, 2013, http://www.st.nmfs.noaa.gov/pls/webpls/MF_ANNUAL_LANDINGS.RESULTS.

202. Ibid.

203. Howard Jacobs, "Crawfish Nabob Tells State of Crustacean," *Times-Picayune*, April 7, 1972.

204. Ibid., "These Governors Are Bought—Not Elected," *Times-Picayune*, March 30, 1961.

205. NOAA, "National Marine Fisheries Annual Commercial Landings Statistics."

206. Paul Rioux, "Flow of Mississippi River Floodwaters through the Morganza Spillway to Increase Gradually," *Times-Picayune*, May 14, 2011.

207. *Teche News*, "State Biologist Spends Two Days in Area Studying Crawfish Situation," May 21, 1959.

208. Blackie Bienvenu, "This and That," *Teche News*, March 19, 1959.

209. Louisiana State University Libraries, "About Percy Viosca Jr.," http://www.lib.lsu.edu/special/viosca/About.html.

210. *Oakland Tribune*, "100 Score of Champ Crawfish Eater," August 8, 1922.

211. Pool, "Vast Commercial Possibilities of the Humble Louisiana Crawfish."

212. Ibid.

213. Ibid.
214. Ibid.
215. Ibid.
216. *Times-Picayune*, "Louisiana Bullfrogs Will Compete in New York Jumping Contest," May 10, 1935.
217. Evelyn E. Jones, "Big Bad Wolf of Bayou at Last Yields Profit," *Times-Picayune New Orleans States Magazine*, May 19, 1940.
218. Percy Viosca Jr., "Crawfish to the Rescue!" *Times-Picayune New Orleans States Magazine*, August 28, 1949.
219. Schoenberger, "Fearless Little Crawfish Supplies Wayside Industry and Affords Family Sport."
220. Percy Viosca Jr., "The Super Crawfish from Pierre Part," *Dixie, Times-Picayune States Roto Magazine*, May 7, 1950.
221. Percy Viosca Jr., "Mudbug Farming," *Louisiana Conservationist* (March 1961).
222. *Teche News*, "State Biologist Spends Two Days in Area Studying Crawfish Situation."
223. Ibid.
224. Ibid.
225. Ibid.

Chapter 6

226. *Port Arthur News*, "Breaux Bridge Cajuns Revolt Against Non-Crawfish World," 1962.
227. Breaux Bridge Crawfish Festival Association, *Crawfish Festival History Records* (Breaux Bridge, 2013).
228. Dormon, *People Called Cajuns*.
229. Gibson, *Archeology and Ethnology*.
230. *Port Arthur News*, "Breaux Bridge Cajuns Revolt Against Non-Crawfish World."
231. *Grit*, "Crawfish Capital of the World," April 27, 1969.
232. Pellerin, Interview.
233. John Lang, "Breaux Bridge Crawfish Event Draws Throng," *Morning Advocate*, April 18, 1968.
234. *Morning Advocate*, "Ashby Landry Revolutionizes Farming of Crawfish," June 25, 1964.
235. *State-Times*, "Breaux Bridge Parade Ends Crawfish Festival," May 16, 1960.
236. *Teche News*, "Thousands Expected to Visit Breaux Bridge for Crawfish Festival," May 12, 1960.
237. Carl Simon, Interview.
238. Ibid.
239. Ibid.
240. Ibid.
241. Ibid.
242. Ibid.
243. Ed Perez, "Breaux Bridge Rings Down Crawfish Festival Curtain," *Morning Advocate*, April 20, 1964.
244. Henry Barousse, "Eating Crawfish," e-mail message to author, July 15, 2013.

245. Howard Jacobs, "Freret Traffic Jam Was Driver Nightmare," *Times-Picayune*, April 29, 1968.

246. John Morris, "Crawfish Festival Attracts Thousands," *Sunday Advocate*, May 5, 1968.

247. Conni Castille and Allison Bohl, *King Crawfish*, DVD Documentary, 2010.

248. *Breaux Bridge, Cecilia, Arnaudville, Parks Telephone Directory* (Breaux Bridge Telephone Company, 1966).

249. Pellerin, Interview.

250. Ibid.

251. Don Hughes, "Only Mud Bugs Mud-Bug Lovers," *Times-Picayune*, April 30, 1972.

252. Pitre, *The Crawfish Book*.

253. Shane K. Bernard, *The Cajuns: Americanization of a People* (Jackson: University Press of Mississippi, 2003).

254. Carl Simon, Interview.

255. Ibid.

256. Carleen Simon, Interview, October 24, 2013.

257. Carl Simon, Interview.

258. Carleen Simon, Interview.

259. Carl Simon, Interview.

260. Ibid.

261. Ibid.

262. *Ruston Daily Leader*, "Crawfish Feast Puts City on World Map," April 28, 1972.

263. Breaux, Interview.

264. Howard Jacobs, "Remoulade: Quiet Descends on 'Crawfish Capital,'" *Times-Picayune*, April 15, 1959.

265. Pellerin, Interview.

266. *Ruston Daily Leader*, "Crawfish Feast Puts City on World Map."

267. Ibid.

268. *Morning Advocate*, "Festivals: Must They Struggle to Survive?" April 20, 1972.

269. Roy Reed, "Cajuns Celebrate Crawfish at an Exuberant Festival in Louisiana," *New York Times*, May 1, 1972.

270. Marcelle B. Wright, "1971 Crawfish Festival Off, Future Festivals in Doubt," *Teche News*, February 28, 1971.

271. Pellerin, Interview.

272. Wright, "1971 Crawfish Festival Off, Future Festivals in Doubt."

273. Kirk Barilleaux, "BB Buys Land for City Park," *Teche News*, October 14, 1971.

274. Hughes, "Only Mud Bugs Mud-Bug Lovers."

275. Ibid.

276. Ibid.

277. Bernard, *The Cajuns*.

278. Ibid.

279. *Teche News*, "Merchants Asked for Cooperation," March 24, 1982.

280. Ibid.

281. Henri C. Bienvenu, "Breaux Bridge Recovering from Festival Invasion," *Teche News*, May 5, 1982.

282. Ibid.

283. *Teche News*, "No Major Problems Despite Big Crowd," May 5, 1982.

284. Carl Simon, Interview.

285. Ibid.

286. Gladys de Villier, "Crawfish Festival Fate Back in Council's Lap," *Teche News*, December 13, 1983.

287. Ibid.

288. *State-Times*, "Crawfish Festival Limited to One Day," December 15, 1983.

289. *Sunday Magazine*, "Art Notes: New Posters," May 20, 1984.

290. Ibid.

291. Kirby Guidry, Interview, September 15, 2013.

292. Breaux Bridge Crawfish Festival Association, *Crawfish Festival History Records*.

293. Gladys de Villier, "In Breaux Bridge, It's Crawfish Time," *State-Times*, May 2, 1986.

294. Ibid.

295. Ibid.

296. Ibid.

297. Smiley Anders, "Smiley Anders' Baton Rouge: Pagans? Us?" *Morning Advocate*, May 15, 1982.

298. Cheryl Albrecht, "Getting to Know You," *Daily Advertiser*, May 29, 1990.

299. Ibid.

300. Ibid.

301. Dominick Cross, "Crawfish Festivities Changing," *The Advocate*, April 29, 1993.

302. Ibid.

303. Pellerin, Interview.

304. Ibid.

305. Carl Simon, Interview.

306. Kenneth LeBlanc, Interview, November 3, 2013.

307. Gladys de Villier, "Downtown Merchants Say Many Visitors Left Angry," *Teche News*, May 5, 1993.

308. Ibid., "Special Traffic Laws for Festival Weekend," *Teche News*, April 28, 1993.

309. Henri C. Bienvenu, "Pense Donc!!" *Teche News*, May 5, 1993.

310. Gladys de Villier, "Breaux Bridge Ready for 'New' Festival," *Teche News*, April 28, 1993.

311. Beverly Corbell, "Breaux Bridge Stews over Crawfish Festival Funding," *Daily Advertiser*, March 11, 2004.

312. Ibid., "Only One Crawfish Festival Remains," *Daily Advertiser*, March 12, 2005.

313. Ibid.

314. Ibid.

315. Ibid.

316. Hudson and Fontenot, *Profitability of Crawfish Peeling Plants*.

317. Bud Lamoreaux, "Woodie's World," *The Funnies* (ESPN Classic, December 25, 2003).

318. *Morning Advocate*, "La. Crawfish Group Names President," May 15, 1965.

319. *Times-Picayune*, "La. Crawfish Meeting Slated," April 30, 1970.

320. Ibid., "LCPA Will Hold Annual Session," September 24, 1974.

321. "Agriculture Today with Commissioner Bob Odom" (Louisiana Department of Agriculture and Forestry, December 14, 1984).

322. *Sunday Advocate*, "Crawfish Show Draws Hundreds to Lafayette," February 5, 1984.
323. Pellerin, Interview.
324. V. Kumar, J. Andrew Petersen and Robert P. Leone, "How Valuable Is Word of Mouth?" *Harvard Business Review*, 2007.
325. David Cheramie, "English to French Translation of Mayor Louis Kern's 1990 *Daily Advertiser*'s Reference to a Bayou Teche Proverb," November 5, 2013; Albrecht, "Getting to Know You."

Chapter 7

326. Viosca Jr., "The Super Crawfish from Pierre Part."
327. Ibid., "Crawfish to the Rescue!"
328. Ibid., "The Super Crawfish from Pierre Part."
329. Ibid.
330. Ibid.
331. *Times-Picayune*, "Crawfish Lack Blamed on Rain," July 24, 1959.
332. Ibid.
333. Pool, "Vast Commercial Possibilities of the Humble Louisiana Crawfish."
334. Ibid.
335. Howard Jacobs, "Crawdad Expert Sees Mudbug Renaissance," *Times-Picayune*, May 25, 1960.
336. Ibid.
337. Guidry, Interview.
338. Ibid.
339. Viosca Jr., "Mudbug Farming."
340. Ibid.
341. Guidry, Interview.
342. Ibid.
343. *Morning Advocate*, "Ashby Landry Revolutionizes Farming of Crawfish.'"
344. Viosca Jr., "Mudbug Farming."
345. Richard T. Lovell (Project Director), "Development of a Crawfish Processing Industry in Louisiana" (Economic Development Administration, U.S. Department of Commerce, March 1968).
346. Hudson and Fontenot, *Profitability of Crawfish Peeling Plants*.
347. Ibid.
348. *State-Times*, "Rep. Angelle Will Seek Crawfish Industry Funds," May 1, 1968.
349. *Morning Advocate*, "LSU Gets $44,000 Grant to Conduct Basic Applied Crawfish Research," May 18, 1966.
350. Tevis, "Tasty Crawfish Dishes Add to Teche Culinary Fame."
351. Viosca Jr., "Mudbug Farming."
352. Ibid.
353. Ibid.
354. Barbara Trahan Broussard, Interview, July 20, 2013.
355. Ibid.
356. Ibid.

357. Ibid.

358. Ibid.

359. Ibid.

360. *Sunday Advocate*, "Crawfish Census Being Taken by Wild Life Dep't," June 4, 1961.

361. Viosca Jr., "Mudbug Farming."

362. Jim Levy, "They're Doing Something About the Crawfish Crop," *Morning Advocate*, March 6, 1960.

363. *Dixie*, "Cultivating the Crawfish," April 10, 1960.

364. Ibid.

365. Levy, "They're Doing Something About the Crawfish Crop."

366. Ibid.

367. Ibid.

368. Ibid.

369. J.S. Badon, "J.S. Badon News of Breaux Bridge," *Teche News*, April 7, 1960.

370. Howard Jacobs, "Mudbugs Are Now in Abundant Supply," *Times-Picayune*, March 24, 1961.

371. Viosca Jr., "Mudbug Farming."

372. Louisiana State University Libraries, "Louisiana Ecology and Conservation: The Percy Viosca Jr. Collection."

373. W. Ray McClain et al., *Louisiana Crawfish Production Manual* (Baton Rouge: Louisiana State University AgCenter, 2007).

374. LSU AgCenter, "2012 LSU AgCenter Agricultural Summary."

375. Robert P. Romaire, "Early Crawfish Extension," e-mail message to author, July 29, 2013.

376. Roland Faulk, Interview, April 4, 2013.

377. Ibid.

378. Ibid.

379. Ibid.

380. Ibid.

381. Ibid.

382. Ibid.

383. Ibid.

384. Romaire, "Early Crawfish Extension."

385. J.G. Broom, "Natural and Domestic Production of Crawfish," *Louisiana Conservationist* (April 1963): 14–15.

386. Ibid.

387. Ibid.

388. Romaire, "Early Crawfish Extension."

389. Lewis Hill and E.A. Cancienne, *Grow Crawfish in Rice Fields* (Baton Rouge: Louisiana State University Agricultural Extension Service, May 1963).

390. Ibid.

391. Ibid.

392. *Sunday Advocate*, "Researcher Seeks to Unlock Louisiana Crawfish's Secrets," October 24, 1965.

393. Ibid.

394. M'Fadden Duffy, "All Outdoors," *Times-Picayune*, May 11, 1966.

395. James W. Avault Jr., *Fundamentals of Aquaculture* (Baton Rouge, LA: AVA Publishing Company Inc., 1996).

396. Robert P. Romaire, "Research," July 30, 2013.

397. James W. Avault Jr., "Louisiana Crawfish," e-mail message to author, November 4, 2013.

398. Ibid.

399. Ibid.

400. Ibid.

401. Ibid.

402. Avault Jr., Interview.

403. Hill and Cancienne, *Grow Crawfish in Rice Fields*.

404. Avault Jr., Interview.

405. Ibid.

406. Fred L. Zimmerman, "Rice Farmers Raise Crawfish in Louisiana Paddies to Lift Income," *Wall Street Journal*, December 10, 1963.

407. Ibid.

408. Ibid.

409. Ibid.

410. NOAA, "National Marine Fisheries Annual Commercial Landings Statistics."

411. Lovell, "Development of a Crawfish Processing Industry in Louisiana."

412. Ibid.

413. *Morning Advocate*, "Louisiana Crawfish Group Plans Industry Promotion," December 18, 1965.

414. Ibid.

415. Faulk, Interview with Roland Faulk.

416. NOAA, "National Marine Fisheries Annual Commercial Landings Statistics."

417. Sherbin Collette, Interview, November 10, 2013.

418. James F. Fowler, Interview, October 31, 2013.

419. Ibid.

420. *Times-Picayune*, "La. Crawfish Meeting Slated," April 30, 1970.

421. Fowler, Interview.

422. Robert P. Romaire, *History and Pioneers in Crawfish Aquaculture*, PowerPoint Presentation (Baton Rouge: Louisiana State University AgCenter, February 24, 2013).

423. Ibid.

424. McClain et al., *Louisiana Crawfish Production Manual*.

425. Avault Jr., Interview.

426. Ibid.

427. Ibid.

428. Ibid.

429. Lamoreaux, "Woodie's World."

430. Ibid.

431. Avault Jr., Interview.

432. LSU AgCenter, *Estimated Louisiana Crawfish Harvest, 1978-2011*, Spreadsheet (LSU Agriculture Center, 2011), http://www.lsuagcenter.

com/NR/rdonlyres/4687F896-C5C5-47D6-A4F4-1F4455760816/88731/
CrawfishHarvestStatistics7812.pdf.

433. Avault Jr., Interview.

434. Ibid.

435. LSU AgCenter, *Estimated Louisiana Crawfish Harvest*.

436. Ibid.

437. Ibid.

438. *Sunday Advocate*, "Crawfish Show Draws Hundreds to Lafayette."

439. Ibid.

CHAPTER 8

440. *State-Times*, "Crawfish Producers Call for Fish-Out," April 28, 1984.

441. LSU AgCenter, *Estimated Louisiana Crawfish Harvest*; NOAA, "National Marine
Fisheries Annual Commercial Landings Statistics."

442. NOAA, "National Marine Fisheries Annual Commercial Landings Statistics."

443. *State-Times*, "Crawfish Producers Call for Fish-Out."

444. Ibid.

445. Ibid.

446. Sherbin Collette, Interview.

447. West Bank Bureau, "Crawfish Strike Success All in the Point of View," *Times-Picayune*, June 24, 1984.

448. Melinda Shelton, "Crawfishermen Defying Basin Ban," *Morning Advocate*, May
15, 1984.

449. "Atchafalaya Crawfishing Continues," *State-Times*, May 3, 1984.

450. Diane Loupe, "Squeeze Play: La. Crawfish Industry in Agony over Prices,"
Times-Picayune, May 7, 1984.

451. West Bank Bureau, "Crawfish Strike Success All in the Point of View."

452. *Morning Advocate*, "Referendum Vote Set for Crawfish Industry," November 12, 1983.

453. Bill Pizzolato, Interview, May 17, 2013.

454. LDAF Press Release Agriculture Today, "Louisiana Cooking Number One in
1985" (Louisiana Department of Agriculture and Forestry, August 16, 1985).

455. Carl Redman, "Restaurants See No Crawfish Industry Glut," *Morning Advocate*,
August 2, 1985.

456. Ibid.

457. *Times-Picayune*, "National Restaurant Chain Orders Crawfish by the Ton,"
May 11, 1985.

458. LDAF Press Release Agriculture Today, "Louisiana Crawfish Wholesalers
Opens" (Louisiana Department of Agriculture and Forestry, February 26, 1987).

459. Ibid.

460. Ibid., "Pillsbury Company Contracts with State's Processors" (Louisiana
Department of Agriculture and Forestry, May 16, 1985).

461. Ibid., "Louisiana's Crawfish Industry Is No Long Just a Seasonal Staple"
(Louisiana Department of Agriculture and Forestry, August 16, 1985).

462. Ibid.

463. Roy Johnson, Interview, November 7, 2013.

464. LDAF Press Release Agriculture Today, "Growth Potential Exists for Crawfish Industry" (Louisiana Department of Agriculture and Forestry, July 27, 1990).

465. Ibid.

466. Ibid.

467. Ibid.

468. Ibid.

469. Ibid.

470. Johnson, Interview.

471. Ibid.

472. Ibid.

473. LDAF Press Release Agriculture Today, "The Reds from the West Are Coming" (Louisiana Department of Agriculture and Forestry, July 31, 1987).

474. Ibid., "Swedish Newspaper: Americans Taking Over" (Louisiana Department of Agriculture and Forestry, August 14, 1987).

475. Johnson, Interview.

476. Reed, *Lâche Pas La Patate*.

477. Mary Foster, "Chinese Crawfish Gracing Menus of Jazz Fest Vendors," *The Advocate*, May 3, 1996.

478. Ibid.

479. Cecil LaCaze, "More About Crawfish," *Louisiana Conservationist*, June 1966.

480. George Henry Penn, "Introduction of American Crawfishes into Foreign Lands," *Ecology* 35, no. 2 (April 1954): 296.

481. Ibid.

482. Ibid.

483. Tetsuya Suko, *Status of Crawfish in Japan* (Urawa, Japan: Saitama Universtiy, 1986).

484. Sidney C.H. Cheung, "Social Life of American Crayfish in Asia" (paper presented at the Globalization, Food and Social Identities in the Asia Pacific Region, ed. James Farrer, Sophia University, Tokyo, February 21, 2009), http://icc.fla.sophia.ac.jp/global%20food%20papers/html/cheung.html.

485. LDAF Press Release Agriculture Today, "La. Businessmen Meet with China Official" (Louisiana Department of Agriculture and Forestry, September 16, 1988).

486. Ibid.

487. Ibid.

488. Jeff Matthews, "'King of Chinese Crawfish' Elton Bernard of Cottonport Dies at Age of 75," *Town Talk*, April 15, 2011.

489. Donna St. George, "Crawfish Wars: Cajun Country vs. China," *New York Times*, May 7, 1997.

490. Matthews, "'King of Chinese Crawfish' Elton Bernard of Cottonport Dies at Age of 75."

491. St. George, "Crawfish Wars: Cajun Country vs. China."

492. LSU AgCenter, *Estimated Louisiana Crawfish Harvest*.

493. Bernard, *The Cajuns*.

494. Ibid.

495. Mary Foster, "Louisiana Crawfish Feeling Pinch at Jazz Fest," *Associated Press*, May 2, 1996.

496. Tom Guarisco, "Sale of Chinese Crawfish Criticized," *The Advocate*, March 18, 1994.

497. Ed Anderson, "Chinese Crawfish Held Up in Label Dispute," *Times-Picayune*, February 8, 1992.

498. Guarisco, "Sale of Chinese Crawfish Criticized."

499. *The Advocate*, "Test Find No Cholera in Chinese Crawfish," September 23, 1997.

500. Patrick Courreges, "Test Finds Drug in Shellfish," *The Advocate*, May 29, 2002.

501. Sherry Sapp, "Top Ag Official Orders Seizure of Crawfish," *The Advocate*, January 27, 1998.

502. Doug Myers, "Senate Panel Nixes Foreign Crawfish Bill," *The Advocate*, June 3, 1992.

503. Marsha Shuler, "No Tales about Tails' Origins," *The Advocate*, May 7, 2008.

504. NOAA, "National Marine Fisheries Annual Commercial Landings Statistics."

505. St. George, "Crawfish Wars: Cajun Country vs. China."

506. Adam Johnson, Interview, November 16, 2013.

507. W. Ray McClain and Robert P. Romaire, "Crawfish Culture: A Louisiana Aquaculture Success Story," *World Aquaculture Society* (2004).

508. St. George, "Crawfish Wars: Cajun Country vs. China."

509. *Times-Picayune*, "Home Cooking—Local Chefs Voice Their Views on Chinese vs. Louisiana Crawfish," September 1, 1996.

510. Mike Urch, "Chinese Crayfish in Short Supply," SeafoodSource.com, August 14, 2011, http://www.seafoodsource.com/en/commentary/seafoodsource-commentary/11068-chinese-crayfish-in-short-supply.

511. D.I. Frugé, Interview, March 5, 2010.

INDEX

ABOUT THE AUTHOR

S am Irwin is a freelance journalist and writer who lives in Baton Rouge. He is the former editor of the *Louisiana Market Bulletin* and served as the press secretary for the Louisiana Department of Agriculture and Forestry. He received his undergraduate and graduate degrees in history from the University of Louisiana at Lafayette in the 1970s. A product of a mixed marriage (his father's family is from north Louisiana, while his mother's is from the heart of French-speaking Louisiana), Irwin's writing showcases the Bayou State.

Irwin's fiction has won several prizes, and his nonfiction work appears regularly in Louisiana newspapers and regional magazines, including *Country Roads*, *The Advocate* and *House and Home*. His writing has also been featured in *Louisiana Kitchen and Culture*, *Louisiana TravelHost*, *Offbeat*, *225*, *Louisiana Film and Video*, *Teche News* and *Louisiana Cookin'*.

His LaNote blog is found at www.LaNote.org.